"*The Communicators* is more than a great business book. It is a moral document – a compelling and necessary roadmap for leadership in the ongoing aftermath of the 2008 economic crisis."

ANASTASIA (STASIA) KELLY
Of Counsel, DLA Piper, and former General Counsel, AIG

"If I were to advise a client in crisis to read just one book before testifying before Congress, or facing a determined regulator, that book would be *The Communicators: Leadership in the Age of Crisis.*"

PAUL BUTLER
Partner, Akin Gump and
former Chief of Staff for Defense Secretary Donald Rumsfeld

"A milestone book that underscores the increasingly critical nexus of social responsibility and sound business practice. Here are invaluably practical lessons on what it really means to do well by doing good."

DR. WILLIAM S. SPEARS
Founder and CEO, Energy Education, Inc.

"*The Communicators* is a blueprint for leadership in an age when even the simplest business decisions seem fraught with liability. One can't help feeling it was written just in the nick of time."

MARTIN D. BEIRNE
Founding Partner of Beirne, Maynard, & Parsons

"A watershed in the literature on leadership. It teaches by example – powerful, riveting examples of men and women who bear the responsibilities of living in a free market and who refuse to hide from crises or take easy ways out."

DR. PHIL BURGESS
President and Senior Fellow, The Annapolis Institute.

"*The Communicators* is a powerfully rendered, indispensable survival manual for a marketplace where digital media make every business decision a potential landmine, and where even proxy statements decisively test leadership."

PAUL FERRILLO
Litigation Counsel, Weil Gotshal

"Leaders must navigate within the critical space where private interests meet public responsibility – where international business, law, politics, and communications inevitably collide.   No other book I've read better describes how a leader can successfully navigate the complexity created by crisis quite as eloquently as *The Communicators*."

THOMAS CAMPBELL
Partner, Pillsbury Winthrop Shaw Pittman, and
former General Counsel of the
National Oceanic and Atmospheric Administration

THE
COMMUNICATORS

THE
COMMUNICATORS

Leadership
In the Age of
Crisis

RICHARD S. LEVICK
WITH CHARLES SLACK

Foreword by Steve Forbes

WATERSHED
PRESS

WATERSHED PRESS
1900 M Street NW
Washington, D.C. 20036

Deisgned by Levick Strategic Communications.
Printed in United States of America.

Library of Congress Cataloging-in-Publication Data has been applied for.

ISBN: 978-09759985-3-3

To my beloved family

CONTENTS

FOREWORD

FOREWORD
By Steve Forbes

In the subtitle of this remarkable book we find two words of obvious and momentous impact: leadership and crisis. The former is something we desperately need, and the latter is the reason that we need it. Yet, as I delved into these rich interviews and commentary, two other fundamental concepts kept coming to mind as integral to any prosperous, free, capitalist democracy: profit and courage.

Profit, though erroneously confused with greed by our system's detractors, is nothing more nor less than the end reward for hard work and vision, which are required to convert good ideas into products or services that others find useful. The benefits of profit are broad and generous. When a company introduces a game-changing innovation after years of backbreaking labor, consumers profit because their lives are enhanced or made easier; employees profit as their wages increase and their jobs become more secure, even as growth based on profit generates new jobs; managers profit as their reputations and compensation swell; other businesses profit as employees and managers of the first company spend their extra capital; the government profits through enhanced tax revenue.

Greed, by contrast, involves taking what does not belong to you or coveting an unreasonable share of existing resources. Greed denies others. While profit creates wealth, greed usurps it. Gordon Gekko, the shady financier of *Wall Street* movie fame, fed anticapitalist opinion with his declaration that greed is good. But Gekko was a criminal, not a capitalist, and he got it precisely wrong.

Greed is bad; profit is good.

The second crucial term, courage, is even weightier than the first because the realization of profit is entirely dependent on courage. If profit is the reward for success in a free-market system, courage is the fuel. Without it, no private enterprise can survive beyond the earliest conceptual phase. It takes courage to risk the time and capital required to start a company, to choose and hire employees capable of helping you achieve your vision and to persevere when others urge you to quit.

Once a company becomes established and successful, the need for courageous leadership is only intensified if the success is to be sustainable. The larger a company becomes, the more complex and nuanced are the demands imposed on its leaders, especially during a crisis. Because human interactions are imperfect, even the best-run companies face crises, often without warning. And at some point in their careers just about all chief executives or board chairmen find themselves making decisions that could determine the success or failure of their enterprise.

As Mr. Levick and Mr. Slack make so clear, the great test lies not in the crisis itself but in the ways we respond. Courage is the moral commitment to keeping a company going through a life-threatening crisis, doing the right thing, and making hard choices when it would be easier and safer to do the opposite. In these pages you'll find powerful examples of corporate leaders summoning the courage to stand by their convictions, to admit their own failings, and to respond to challenges with honesty and candor rather than secrecy. Some of these corporate leaders will already be well-known to you. Others deserve to be.

Leadership today is tied as never before to effective communications. In an age of instant global transmission of words and images, a secret at 11:45 a.m. can be a global scandal by noon, replete with streaming videos and countless critics weighing in from every corner. In such a world, you, as the corporate leader, must more than ever before find the courage to serve as the unwavering public face of your company, the surest voice in communicating its values and objectives.

The experiences and observations in this book, presented as "rules" of leadership, will help you become a better and more thoughtful leader and more effective steward of your company. That, in and of itself, is important. Yet history has also placed on today's corporate leaders an even graver responsibility – to be those vigilant stewards of capitalism at a time when our system is under the greatest attack in generations.

The attack is coming from within. As the developing world – from China to India to Vietnam to Brazil – unabashedly embraces various forms of capitalism as the surest way to bring prosperity to their people, many here in the birthplace of modern capitalism are questioning whether the system has run its course. It's fashionable to advocate for greater protections for the public from the purported ravages and excesses of capitalism. As a result, every executive who mistakes profit for greed or takes the easy way out of a crisis at the expense of employees or the public adds one more arrow to the quiver of those who would replace capitalism with ever more overreaching government controls.

Make no mistake: asking whether capitalism should survive is the same thing as asking whether freedom should survive. In our recent book, *How Capitalism Will Save Us*, Elizabeth Ames and I laid out a case for capitalism, not as the devil's bargain its apologists claim it to be (a sort of necessary accommodation to the realities of human greed), but as the most moral system that humankind has ever developed. If free speech guarantees the right to *express* one's ideas, capitalism affords one the right to *act* on those ideas, to put private capital and resources to work in pursuit of an individual or common goal. Without capitalism, freedom is a parlor game.

Yet our very declaration that "capitalism will save us" prompts the vital question: who will save capitalism?

The answer: those leaders who understand and accept the costs and responsibilities that go hand in hand with the rewards of free markets, those who find the *courage* to *profit* with integrity. Read this book and ask yourself that same question: who will save capitalism?

I believe that you will.

SECTION ONE

THE BLIND SPOT

The woman needed some air. As division manager for a company mired in a deep financial crisis, she'd been working day and night for months. Even when she tried to sleep, some midnight emergency inevitably summoned her to her Blackberry or back to the office. One afternoon, with the walls closing in, she stripped off the portable devices that clung to her like electronic barnacles and rode the elevator to the ground floor.

Outside, the warm sun on her face, boats on the river, cabs honking, and pedestrians passing by without a thought to her company's woes, all helped the woman put things in perspective. One way or another, the crisis would end and life would go on. On the way back to the office, she decided to treat herself to a cookie at a nearby bakery. Then she thought: why not spread the cheer around?

"Give me every cookie and brownie in the store," she told

the surprised clerk.

Back at the office, she wandered her floor like Santa, dispensing goodies from an enormous white box. At first, her gesture had precisely the effect on her overworked team members that she had hoped. The first smiles she'd seen in ages greeted her at every desk and cubicle she passed.

And then one worker who had been away from his desk and missed the fun found the empty box sitting on a table in the lunchroom.

He asked, "Why no cookie for me?"

Not content just to share his displeasure verbally, the man filed a *formal written complaint* with the company's internal investigations department, charging that he'd been the victim of a deliberate slight. The complaint went nowhere, of course – they were only cookies! And the woman had paid for them herself. But by then this small act of spontaneous generosity had backfired, only adding more pollution to the company's toxic atmosphere.

Now, a dispute over snacks is something you might expect at a daycare center rather than an office full of grownups. But, as with most cases where minor annoyances get blown out of proportion, the cookie wasn't really the problem at all.

The underlying problem in this story (which is true, although we've masked the identity of the company) was a *scarcity mentality* that the company's senior management had allowed to develop from the very start of the crisis, through one missed leadership opportunity after another.

Consider the mood at most companies when a crisis first erupts. People naturally want to believe in their company, its mission, its strength, and its leadership. They come together, assuring themselves and one another: *we're all in this together; we'll get through this; we have what it takes; we're strong enough to survive if we work together.* This period of *abundance mentality*, when optimism still prevails, is the most crucial time in a crisis, when top executives have the best (sometimes, the only) chance to put the company on track to recovery and renewed prosperity. Alas, that window of opportunity has shrunk dramatically in an age of instant global communications. These days, effective response is measured in hours rather than days.

The chief executive of the company in question had an opportunity to emerge as just such a leader. A brilliant businessman with a sterling record, he might have played to his natural abilities, communicating his vision for recovery in bold terms to the public and to his employees. People want leaders. In a time of crisis, they practically beg for them. Yet the CEO was cautious, advised by attorneys not to speak out too forcefully, for fear he would put himself in jeopardy. About the only view the employees or the public had of this very capable man was when he testified in government hearings, always on the defensive as politicians vying for the next headline peppered him with loaded questions. He maintained this defensive posture even as public opinion swirled and everyone from bloggers to reporters to activists began telling the company's story in the most unflattering light.

This almost-leader had plenty of company as the financial crisis swept the country in late 2008. While everyone loves a lofty title and the perks that go with it, what became painfully clear was how few individuals were willing and prepared to step forward as true leaders. The fact is that most of us are not constituted to lead.

Even natural leaders often don't seek the opportunity to prove themselves. Captain Chesley Sullenberger certainly had no leadership heroics in mind in January 2009 when he climbed into the cockpit of that US Airways jet he famously glided to a safe landing on the Hudson River a few minutes after takeoff. In every sense, he was a reluctant hero who performed brilliantly. Leaders of corporations may never have to land a plane on the Hudson, but the decisions they make (or refuse to make) when a crisis arises can have every bit as great an impact on the life or death of a corporation.

This book is about leadership in its many, many incarnations. It is about how crises test that leadership and, perhaps more important, how strong, visible leadership prevents crises from occurring.

In the absence of such strong, visible leadership, employees working under extreme pressure begin to lose their sense of cohesiveness and their eagerness to sacrifice for the greater good of the company. Amid whispers and rumors about who will be the next to get axed and when, the abundance mentality is quickly replaced by its opposite, the scarcity mentality. That's when people stop bleeding corporate colors and just start bleeding. That's when they stop laboring over your company's mission statement or gracefully crafted press release and start laboring over their resume. Selfishness replaces sacrifice. One thinks more about protecting a job or a department than protecting the company's reputation.

Then one day you have a man in a lunchroom staring at an empty box and saying, "Why no cookie for me?"

---------- **Rule No. 1** ----------

Learn to Accept Death
Do Not Go Quietly into the Ink Black Night

Naval aviators dream of the sort of flying conditions that Charles W. "Willy" Moore awoke to one warm January morning in 1972, sunny skies, clear visibility, and calm waters stretching out as far out on the Gulf of Tonkin as he could see. Considering that Moore was about to engage in one of the most dangerous activities on earth – flying a combat mission over Vietnam from the deck of an aircraft carrier – this day was as good as it gets.

Moore's high spirits lasted just a few seconds after takeoff from the deck of the *USS Constellation*. It was then that the engine of his A-7 Corsair jet failed, transforming in a split-second his mission from one of attack to a struggle to survive.

"The best way I can describe it is as peaks of agony and ecstasy," Moore says now. "There's stark, raving, gut-grinding agony when you realize that the airplane is going to crash into the ocean and you've got to get out. The big unknown is, will my ejection seat work? If it doesn't, I'm a dead man.

"You pull the ejection and it is sheer ecstasy when you realize that the seat is firing and you're going to get out. But then you have the agony of, is my parachute going to open? When it does, there is ecstasy again. Then, is my flotation gear going to work or am I going to drown? And the flotation gear works and you're as happy as you can be. All of this takes place in nanoseconds. But your mind speeds up and you see every detail."

Before reaching the safety of a helicopter, he had to use a pair of handguns to ward off Chinese fishermen – known for abducting downed American pilots – and then jump into water just after a shark had brushed past his raft. The entire ordeal took less than half an hour and left him uninjured but physically and emotionally exhausted. Flight surgeons prescribed a little brandy and a good night's rest. The next day he suited up, climbed in a cockpit, and flew again.

It's a little glib to refer to such an experience as another day at the office for a carrier pilot. Yet hazardous missions, engine failures, and landings on ink-black nights were so common that Moore and his fellow pilots had a special name for those times when the margin between life and death narrowed to a razor's edge: *on government time.*

"It was the euphemism for, 'My life's on the line...I'm willing to do it...this is what's expected of me...if I buy the farm, so be it,'" says Moore. In other words, mission success required setting aside very real and natural fears of mortality in order to accomplish something you had decided was bigger than yourself.

"That is a very liberating feeling, by the way," he adds. "If you can overcome the fear of dying, you can perform at a level that you otherwise couldn't get close to."

In fact, Moore performed at that level through 40 years in the U.S. Navy, rising to the rank of Vice Admiral before retiring at 58 in 2004 to enter private business. In the end, he chalked up 220 combat missions in Vietnam and 1,001 total carrier landings, placing him in the select rank of a few dozen legendary carrier pilots with a thousand or more missions.

Assuming such stratospheric risk has as much to do with passion as profession. Moore traces his own passion for flying back to his father, Charles Moore Sr., who flew B-17 bombers during World War II. "As with a lot of the old World War II guys, you'd never know it if you walked into our house or talked to him," Moore recalls. "It wasn't something he talked about."

But Charles Sr. had a way of communicating a whole lot in a very few words.

When his father made clear that Moore would have to find a way to finance college on his own, Moore, an excellent high school student and athlete in Missouri, gravitated to the military academies. Accepted by each one of them, he was leaning towards the Air Force and asked his father's advice. "I'll never lose my appreciation of this one comment he made that shaped my life," Moore recalls. "He said, 'I always admired those Navy guys that flew off aircraft carriers. In my opinion, that's the pinnacle of flying.' That's all it took."

The U.S. Naval Academy proved to be a supremely demanding environment. "We started out with 1,500 guys, but by the time the first summer ended we'd lost 300 or 400 of them. It was a tough place. In those days, they didn't care if they graduated only one guy. They were going to know that one guy was pretty tough," Moore says. "But I took to it. I loved it. It was a great place to go to school…They immerse you into this Navy culture and it gets into your blood."

History placed Moore and his fellow fliers in harm's way right from the start. He graduated from the academy in 1968, at the zenith of the air war in Vietnam. For a young pilot eager to test his mettle in combat, he could not have chosen a more propitious time.

Like many men of exceptional courage, Moore tends to downplay personal heroics. "Once you're into it and you begin this very methodical training process, it becomes very technical and it becomes part of your personal capability," he says.

But there was one aspect of the job that no amount of training or experience could make routine – the night landing.

"The nighttime at sea is totally black. There is no horizon. If you have a clear night with a full moon and stars, you might see a little faint horizon out there. That's a real joy and a gift," Moore says. "But most nights are as black as can be. You're on instruments from the minute you sit down in the jet until you get back to your room aboard ship."

In fact, one Navy study found that aviators' heart rates were actually lower during combat than during night landings. "You know you can do it, but every night you go out there, you're saying, 'I wonder if I'll be at peak performance tonight,'" recalls Moore. "Am I going to be a little lethargic? Am I going to be unfocused?'

"I have seen guys over the years walk up to the flight deck on a dark, stormy night, when the ship's moving, and they walk right back down to the ready room and say, 'I'm done.' That's the end of your Navy career. Being a Navy pilot is voluntary. You don't have to do it. I made a career decision every time I stepped up on a flight deck at night."

But he kept flying long after Vietnam. In 1986, Moore led a squadron of fighters knocking out air defense systems in the raid on Libya. His last mission, at 47, came in May 1993 when, as an air wing commander, he landed his F/A-18 Hornet on the deck of the *USS Theodore Roosevelt* during a tour of the Mediterranean. "That tour scared me to death because I felt like my immortality was running out on me," Moore recalls. "When I got out of the Navy, there was nobody with more flight time, and I was probably the most combat-experienced guy, or close to it. But there was this gremlin on my shoulder saying, 'Buddy, you know, your time is running out. We haven't been able to kill you in the last 25 years but by God we're going to get you on this tour.'"

When the gremlins speak, it's time to listen. He assumed leadership roles in the Navy. Vice Admiral Moore served as Deputy Chief of Naval Operations, Fleet Readiness and Logistics and Commander of U.S. Naval Forces Central Command and Commander, U.S. Fifth Fleet.

In 2004, Moore decided to try his leadership skills in a whole new environment: corporate America. He joined defense contractor Lockheed-Martin and in August 2009 became the first CEO of Lockheed's United Arab Emirates division. The UAE is a major Lockheed customer, purchasing sophisticated F-16 fighter jets, C-130 transport planes, and missile defense systems.

One thing that has surprised Moore is the level of challenge in translating military leadership skills into the business world. The difficulty does not reflect weakness in either system; instead, he believes, the two worlds present inherently different strengths and objectives. The military is designed around completing specific missions. "This creates a distinct unity of command and unity of effort," Moore says. "It's very clear who is leading and what the mission is. It's clear to every person in the organization."

In that environment, considerations such as financial efficiency and personal reward take back seats to the collective goal of accomplishing the vital task at hand.

"The military is structured to optimize leadership. It's underpinned by the Uniform Code of Military Justice. It's law. If you're in the military, you take an oath to obey," Moore says. "You don't have to like your boss or respect your boss, but by golly you've got to follow him if he gives you a lawful order. There's a leadership ethos in the military, but also what I'll call a 'followship' ethos. People follow their leaders."

Corporations operate in an entirely different realm. The most successful among them, including Moore's own Lockheed-Martin, are supremely adapted to the overriding priorities of maximizing efficiency and financial returns. He describes corporations as "matrix organizations" in which individual departments or managers compete to produce the best numbers and measure success by personal performance or the performance of their departmental silos. "Matrix organizations exist in business for very good reasons," Moore says. "They are superb in their potential to create efficiency or reduce resource requirements."

At the same time, it's that very matrix structure that presents CEOs with leadership challenges that can sometimes be greater and more complex than those faced by military commanders. "Leadership in the military is much more straightforward," Moore says. If you walk into a meeting with a certain rank and with combat ribbons on your chest, you make an unspoken declaration of your credentials in a way that a gray flannel suit simply does not.

In an environment where command is less structurally ordained, effective leadership more than ever demands that the chief executive lead by persuasion and example. Here, Moore refers again to that trait that's as valuable in the boardroom or corner office as it is in the cockpit of a jet preparing to catapult into combat: the ability to fly "on government time."

While CEOs don't face the prospect of being blown out of the sky by a surface-to-air missile, they do fear the prospect of a sort of death of the ego for failing in the corporate environment. "If I have one criticism of some executives I've seen, it's that they are way too egotistical," Moore says. "If they would leave their egos at the front door when they come to work every day, my sense is they'd be a helluva lot more successful. They'd be willing to take more risks." Only by overcoming the fear of damage to one's ego can a person take the risks necessary to best achieve the mission that's crucial for the organization.

After completing a successful carrier mission, Moore would

sometimes hear a colleague praise him for behaving fearlessly.

"In my heart I did not feel that I was fearless," he recalls. "But I had figured one thing out: I was committed to the mission, and I was absolutely going to do it. I was on government time."

During a crisis, the horizon traditionally disappears and many corporations lose their bearings. In order to win, the first step is to overcome the fear of failure, of a corporate death, and go boldly into that dark night. Determine if sacrifices must be made and, if so, make them early. Bleeding must be stopped, silos must work as a team, and crisis teams must focus on the battle *and* the war. This is a book about learning to win both.

RULE No. 2

GET CAUGHT IN THE ACT OF LEADERSHIP

Lessons From the House of Morgan

No one ever said it better than Tom Hoog, former chairman of the global public relations firm, Hill & Knowlton, and a veteran of many crisis situations. His advice to anyone running a company or serving a client or forging public policy: *"Get caught in the act of leadership."*

As of this writing, it is still uncertain which, if any, public sector or private sector kingpins will soon be happily ensnared in just such bold acts amid persistent economic crisis. The good news is that history provides ample instances of similar challenges well-met by men and women of action. The situational details are always different, but the details that define leadership do not change.

The current financial crisis has, for example, drawn comparison to the Panic of 1907. As would happen a century later, public confidence in the financial markets plummeted,

the money supply dried up, and even healthy businesses could not obtain credit to prosper and grow. Then, as now, some observers questioned whether American-style capitalism had run its course.

When that crisis erupted, John Pierpont Morgan, head of the Morgan banking empire, took charge. Although 70 and semi-retired, Morgan, over the course of two harrowing weeks in the fall of 1907, led teams of bankers and the Treasury Secretary in one ad hoc effort after another to create liquidity and stop the panic. He raised money to rescue trust companies, the New York Stock Exchange, and the City of New York. At the end of those two weeks, he summoned the presidents of the financial institutions that were at the core of the trouble, the trust companies, to his private library on East 36th Street in Manhattan. The meeting lasted nearly all night. By 4 a.m. Morgan had secured an agreement from the presidents to supply a final infusion of capital that would stop the run on the trusts. This extraordinary private initiative averted the crisis and ultimately led to the formation of the Federal Reserve.

In today's more complex, global, and regulated economy, it's unlikely that any private individual could exert the influence that J.P. Morgan did in ending the panic more than a century ago. Our world is ruled by litigation, legislation, and regulation. The lessons Morgan offers for today relate not to the specifics of his actions but to the nature of his leadership.

"Morgan had astonishing self-confidence, even as a young man," says Jean Strouse, author of *Morgan: American Financier* and the most authoritative living source on the man. When he was about 11, a teacher threw him out of class for laughing. Instead of feeling guilty or sad, Morgan went home and wrote an outraged letter reprimanding the teacher.

"As Henry Adams said of Theodore Roosevelt, Morgan was

pure *act*," Strouse notes. "He could often size up a situation or a deal or a person almost instantly, and take quick action. Most of the time, he would not have been able to tell you why he did what he did. He just did it. That was true in 1901 when he put together U.S. Steel in 12 weeks, and it was true in 1907."

Central to Morgan's willingness to act decisively was his willingness to risk his reputation. Despite a lifetime of spectacular successes, his reputation might have suffered irreparable harm had he tried and failed to stop the1907 panic. Did Morgan care? "I would bet that he didn't even think about the effect on his reputation," Strouse says. "There was a crisis, he had a tremendous understanding of financial markets, he trusted himself to make up solutions as he went along, thought that no one else was in position to take command, and that doing nothing would be a disaster. He was not thinking about how his actions would go down in history. That quality, that natural assumption of command, tends to inspire trust. Other bankers and many political leaders on both sides of the Atlantic trusted Morgan."

Even Morgan could not have stopped the panic by himself. While making the ultimate decisions about which financial institutions to save, Morgan relied heavily on information and recommendations gathered by able young lieutenants and on the steady counsel of two senior banking colleagues, George Banker of the First National Bank and James Stillman of National City Bank.

He also knew that acting decisively meant being ruthless where necessary. The head of the failed Knickerbocker Trust, Charles Barney, was an old friend of Morgan's. Yet when Morgan's advisors informed him that they did not have time to ascertain whether the company was strong enough to merit a bailout before its panicked depositors drew its cash down to zero, Morgan cut Knickerbocker loose, let it fail, and moved on to the next teetering domino. Barney committed suicide in the wake of the failure.

Morgan didn't seek out crises and, especially in his later years, privately complained to friends that he was not being left alone to travel and collect art. "But I think he actually loved being at the center of the action," Strouse says, "being the man people turned to in a crisis. It's a pretty heady experience. Morgan spent his life studying financial markets. He had amassed reserves and worked to head off other panics in the past. When the big crisis of 1907 blew up, he had all the right knowledge and instincts."

Morgan didn't wait around to see which way the wind was blowing or form a committee to explore options. He knew that times of pure crisis called for pure action.

──────────── **RULE No. 3** ────────────

HARD WORK AND THE RIGHT LEADER WIN MORE OFTEN THAN TALENT

A Diamond is a Lump of Coal That Was Persistent

──────────────────────────────────

History records the 2002 Winter Olympics in Salt Lake City as a resounding American success story. U.S. athletes, not usually dominant in winter competition, won 34 total medals, second only to Germany's 36, including 10 gold medals, third behind Norway and Germany. Staged just a few months after the 9/11 terrorist attacks, the games offered two weeks of joy and patriotic healing for a wounded nation.

The success was especially remarkable considering that, just a few years earlier, the Salt Lake City Olympics were mired in one of the worst scandals in the history of the games.

In the late 1990s, charges surfaced that members of the Salt Lake Organizing Committee had bribed International Olympic Committee (IOC) officials to vote in their city as host. Some of those officials resigned in the wake of the allegations. The scandal was so tainting that private donations, crucial to U.S. Olympic efforts, began to dry up. Some questioned whether the games would go on at all.

Dick Schultz, then executive director of the United States Olympic Committee (USOC), had served as a Division I basketball coach at the University of Iowa, athletic director at The University of Virginia and Cornell University, and as head of the NCAA. Now this major crisis shadowed the final chapters of his storied career. "This was one of those things you get into and all of a sudden – boom!" Schultz recalls.

To be sure, the USOC was not implicated in the bribery accusations, and Schultz, in any event, had come on board after Salt Lake City was awarded the games. Even so, the USOC was directly involved in choosing Salt Lake City, while any scandal involving the Olympics was a potential disaster for the U.S. governing body.

To help guide the USOC through the crisis, Schultz relied on principles of leadership and communications learned and tempered through years of coaching. It's when things begin to fall apart at the seams that you're best advised to rely on the fundamentals that first made you strong. One jump shot won't turn around a losing season, and one quick-fix gesture or pronouncement won't turn around a crisis. What is needed is clear vision and people with the mental toughness and persistence to show up day after day with the best they have to offer.

As a basketball coach, Schultz could not himself block shots or sink free throws. So he quickly learned the importance of identifying a go-to player persistently willing to take control on the court and lead the team by example.

"In basketball you need that floor leader, those playmakers who are ready to take things into their own hands when things go bad," Schultz says. "They have to be willing to challenge their teammates."

Often, these playmakers are not the most gifted athletes. At Iowa, Schultz saw some of the most naturally talented shooters plateau at certain levels of proficiency but never emerge as stars. "They couldn't get over the hump. They couldn't push themselves hard enough or be competitive enough to get themselves to the next level where their talents would fully blossom. But then you had others with less talent who were so highly motivated that they would just push, push, push, work, work, work, and perform far above their potential and be much better team players."

His favorite example was Don Nelson, a member of the Iowa team when Schultz first arrived as an assistant coach in 1960. "He didn't have all the skills others did, but he was a hard worker and committed and ended up being very productive." Nelson, who went on to a legendary career with the perennial champion Boston Celtics before turning to coaching, "just had this strong work ethic. He knew he had to perfect every skill."

Now, Schultz understood that the USOC would need a field general to take over as chief executive of the Salt Lake Organizing Committee, someone who could assume the daily pressures and decisions – someone who, again, would be tirelessly *persistent*. The committee found its playmaker in future Massachusetts governor and entrepreneur Mitt Romney. Voters may debate Romney's virtues as a political candidate, but there's little debate that he was the committed star needed to help rescue the Salt Lake games from disaster.

Romney's executive flair, and his willingness to take calculated risks, helped turn the situation in Salt Lake City around. A Mormon and graduate of Brigham Young, he was able to speak directly with the people in Utah and regain their trust and support. More crucially, Romney was committed body and soul to the process. Like Don Nelson, he recognized what was at stake in the contest at hand, and he devoted himself 100 percent to the success of the team, Schultz says.

Other key figures emerged. Several Salt Lake Organizing Committee and USOC staffers redoubled their efforts to make the games a success. Then-Utah Gov. Michael Leavitt became an active and vocal leader, working with Romney and the USOC to rehabilitate the public image of the Utah games. Schultz also cites Bill Hybl, then the USOC volunteer president, as a vital ally. And, in another crucial initiative, the USOC created an ethics panel to publicly investigate the scandal, naming George Mitchell, the former Maine senator and widely admired diplomat and statesman, to head the investigation.

Schultz knew from experience how important open, candid communications were to any team, not just among the players but for the greater community of supporters as well. Boosters who write checks and fans expected to fill seats in the coliseum don't need to know the playbook or every facet of the game plan, but they do need enough information to trust the integrity of the competition. In this case, the extended team amounted to the entire United States if not the world.

"We had to communicate in a meaningful way. That meant being up front about the issues, not trying to hide anything, and making sure everything was out there," Schultz says. "That's the only way you're going to solve the problem. You've got to raise billions of dollars to run the Olympics. You have to do that through sponsorships and marketing. If you have something that people don't trust, they're not going to put their money into it."

The USOC hired an independent law firm to investigate the scandal and provided regular progress reports to the media and the public.

Finally, as he crafted a comprehensive public relations response to the scandal, Schultz leveraged the value the public puts on how individual athletes train and strive to compete on the world stage. "We put together a strong public relations program emphasizing Olympic athletes," says Schultz. "This whole [scandal] wasn't about athletes. That involved other people and other situations that the athletes had no control over. We stressed that the United States, and corporations, needed to support these wonderful athletes who were working 24/7 to prepare for the Olympics," Schultz says. "That campaign was very, very successful."

During the height of the scandal, the thought of just breaking even seemed like a distant dream. Yet, in the end, the Salt Lake City games turned a profit of just over $100 million.

Of all the coaching fundamentals that Schultz found useful during the crisis, perhaps most helpful was his ability honed over the years to be comfortable making decisions in a spotlight, even at the risk of being wrong. "As a coach, I would many times have a split-second opportunity to make a decision where, if that decision was wrong, there were 16,000 people [in the stands] who knew it right away, and a couple of million others watching television.

"The main part is you've got to be comfortable in your own skin, and you have to have a good level of mental and emotional stability to handle a crisis. And you have to have people who will support you."

─────── RULE NO. 4 ───────
LEADERSHIP IS VISIBLE MOTION
Action Without Communication Equals Inaction & Weakness

One of the most difficult problems executives face during crises is confronting the fact that a crisis actually exists, according to Harvey L. Pitt, Chief Executive of Kalorama Partners, a business consultancy based in Washington. That's not as obvious as it may seem. "People can be very good at persuading themselves that things aren't as bad as they actually are," says Pitt.

In Pitt's own case, history provided no such opportunity for self-deception when his greatest leadership crisis, as Chairman of the Securities and Exchange Commission, coincided with the terrorist attacks of Sept. 11, 2001. To be sure, the existence of a crisis was never in doubt. As chairman of the body charged with protecting investors and maintaining orderly and efficient markets, his position was especially sensitive given that the attacks were tantamount to a concerted assault on American financial might. Barely a month into his job when the planes struck the World Trade Center, Pitt had to balance the conflicting need of reopening the markets as quickly as possible in order to demonstrate resolve and confidence against the need to prevent further damage and chaos should the markets reopen too soon.

Pitt understood, viscerally, the need to make decisions as close to Ground Zero as he could get, rather than from SEC headquarters in Washington. "When a crisis has a location, it's absolutely essential for a leader to be onsite. If not, you will be perceived as not really a part of the fray. What you cannot do is allow others to see you as aloof or outside the daily efforts to slog through the crisis. You have to be seen with your troops, being very much a part of the activity and working just as hard as everyone alongside of you." The day after the attacks, as quickly as travel restrictions allowed, Pitt moved his base to New York, where he remained for the immediate duration of the crisis.

Note Pitt's conscious emphasis on the importance, not just of acting during a crisis, but of *being seen* as acting. That's more than just image or ego talking; it is the realization that the essence of leadership is the effect you have on others. "The worst sin in a crisis is to create the impression of inaction. Inaction is often misinterpreted as a lack of concern or lack of confidence or will. Any of those readings is very, very dangerous," Pitt says.

"We had constant lines of communication with various exchanges, the investment banking community, the Federal Reserve, the president's working group on the financial markets, the White House, and members of Congress," Pitt recalls. He spent days meeting with New York politicos and financial executives, and talking with leaders of the rescue efforts at Ground Zero.

Just as important was the line of communication he kept open with the SEC's largest constituency – the American public, grappling at once with shock and grief for the nation, as well as very real and very personal fears about what the disaster might mean for their own financial lives and savings.

"After our meetings each day, we held press conferences… because, if you are not accessible and people don't know for certain what you are doing or have decided not to do, they will speculate. And speculation will produce erroneous conclusions, which will, in turn, produce panic, fear, and resentment.

"You have to make sure the press is adequately informed. That means you have to put up with questions – sometimes very hard and difficult questions you might prefer not to have been asked."

As part of the communications plan, the SEC actively solicited public comments and suggestions for how to deal with the crisis. While each crisis and organization will present different needs and approaches, Pitt believes that soliciting opinions from a wide variety of constituents is vital to calming their worst fears and conjectures.

"People want to feel that there's somebody in charge, which is very important, and also want to know that, if they do have thoughts, ideas, or concerns, they can communicate them to government leaders and have their views considered," Pitt says. "You occasionally can receive a real gem of an idea [that way], but the most important reason for utilizing such a process isn't simply to receive occasional gems; it's to make it clear to people that you know they have an interest in what is transpiring, you know they're worried about where things might be going, and you want them to have a mechanism for weighing in."

The need for action does not justify rash action. Naturally and understandably, there were intense pressures on Pitt and others to re-open the nation's securities markets immediately. "People wanted to demonstrate to the terrorists that they couldn't keep our system down for very long. That was very understandable," Pitt says.

Yet, there were compelling reasons to pursue a more prudent schedule. First and foremost, was the possibility that the physical consequences of reopening the New York, American, and NASDAQ Stock Exchanges would recommence a daily influx of large numbers of people to the financial center, potentially interfering with rescue efforts still underway just steps away at Ground Zero.

Second, if the markets were immediately reopened, but could not function properly, they might be forced to shut down again. Pitt believed that such an occurrence would destroy public confidence in our markets and send a message far more damaging to the country and encouraging to our enemies than any message inevitably associated with allowing the markets to stay closed a few more days.

When the markets eventually opened on Monday, Sept. 17, six days after the attacks, they handled unprecedented trading volume. As expected, stock prices initially dropped substantially amid investor concerns about the liquidity of their investments after a six-day market closure. Yet the markets did not falter in handling the huge trading volume and, in fact, soon rebounded, reinforcing the wisdom of the decision to delay.

Also, the decision to prudently defer the reopening of the markets could not be seen as inaction because Pitt had carefully and publicly laid out the reasons behind the decision. It was something everyone could understand.

Implicit in the necessity to act promptly, even though you don't yet have all the facts at hand, is the willingness to recognize (painfully and, if necessary, publicly) that you may make some decisions that prove ill-advised, provided you also act promptly to correct any missteps.

"Dynamic decision-making means you have to stand watch," says Pitt. "You can't take action or approach a problem with a course of conduct and then rest on your laurels. You have to ask, continuously, is this working? Have we made things better or are we making things worse, and what are the trends?"

When necessary, admit you've taken a wrong turn, correct the error, and move on. "There's nothing wrong with that. People may want to criticize you, but that's a risk you have to accept," Pitt says.

When a crisis strikes, any thoughtful leader naturally wants to gather as much information as possible before making the decisions likely to impact people's lives and careers. In the end, true leadership involves understanding that you will face the most important decisions of your career with *incomplete* information and accepting the responsibility to make those decisions anyway.

"In a crisis, there is no absolute truth. All truth is relative. You make decisions based on the best available information you have, plus the best input you can get. But at some point, you've got to make the decision," Pitt says. "There are those who want to be certain that they're doing all the right things. The problem is that people watching the crisis unfold need the assurance and comfort of knowing that leaders are dealing with the crisis in real time."

RULE No. 5

RISKING IT ALL CAN BE THE LEAST RISKY OPTION

Changing the Game Down Under

When he was asked in 2005 to shake up Telstra, Australia's state-owned telecommunications giant struggling to compete in a deregulated telecommunications market, Sol Trujillo knew he would face stiff challenges from those who favored the status quo.

Trujillo arrived with a record of innovation and achievement at the helm of such prominent American and European companies as US West, Inc., one of the original Baby Bells, and Orange, the multinational wireless giant – and a reputation as an effective and financially savvy manager, as well as one of his industry's pioneers in market-based management. "Still," Trujillo recalls, "there was a lot of conversation about, 'why do we need an American CEO coming to run this iconic Australian company?'"

Even before his arrival, it was clear there were going to be barriers and roadblocks over and above the challenge of transforming a moribund, government-controlled business into a high-performing enterprise with world-leading results.

As with most companies with a history of comfortable government-protected monopoly status, Telstra's culture of entrenched power and insulated silos that looked first to government and only later to the customer, was its greatest impediment to success in a competitive market. The board, to its credit, recognized this fact. "I was asked to come down to Australia as a change agent. I was recruited by the board to transform the company from one that was government-focused to one that was market–based. We had to turn it into a competitive business because it had lost market share in every major category since competition began in the 1990s. Shareholders, battered by share prices that had fallen more than 40 percent off their highs, demanded a turnaround and the promise of better performance."

What the company desperately needed, Trujillo believed, was a differentiating strategy anchored by a game-changing achievement that would be at once practical and yet highly symbolic of what he described as the New Telstra – the world's first fully-integrated, media-communications company. One of the initial steps in the strategy was to launch Australia's first nationwide mobile Internet – an advanced, high-speed broadband wireless network that would reach more than 99 percent of the people in Australia and would rival or surpass the best wireless networks in the world. The nationwide wireless deployment had a $1 billion price tag – a big bet and a huge risk, especially given the nation's immense geography and low population density.

Instead of the three or four years that most companies would devote to such an ambitious project, Trujillo challenged his team to complete the job in a year. They did it in 10 months. This game-changing initiative was conceived to delight customers, stun competitors, and demonstrate the convenience and potential of high-speed mobile communications to everyone – including business and government users. Though the risks were great, Trujillo also knew that the greatest risk for Telstra at this crucial juncture in its history would be to *fail* to undertake a game-changing initiative that would advance the nation's economy and generate measureable returns in a marketplace where consumers would buy it, use it, and stay with it.

"We figured out how to turn three years into one year. Instead of designing, contracting, and building seriatim, we followed parallel paths to turn three years into one," he recalls. "When you break all the paradigms of how to plan and execute, you have shareholders who are happy, you have customers with assets that no other consumers have, and you have employees saying to themselves, 'We did it!' In fact, the employees discovered they could do world-leading work as they built a world-leading mobile Internet under budget and with time to spare."

In October 2006, Telstra rolled out its new, world-class network, which now delivers information at network speeds of up to 21 megabits per second (Mbps) nationwide and 42 Mbps in major metropolitan areas. Each extra megabit makes it that much easier and faster to transmit videos, text, or even vital medical scans wherever they're needed. More speed means more convenience, more choices, and more control for consumers and enterprise users alike. Hence, Telstra provided mobile Internet speeds in 2008 that doubled or tripled the 2010 aspirations of most of its peers around the globe.

As Trujillo pushed innovation in technology, he also

introduced market-based management, new business support systems, and performance-based management, which permitted the company to become leaner by shedding about 20 percent of its workforce – no easy task in a culture accustomed to management complacency and lifetime employment. "We imposed benchmarks and introduced a Learning Academy. Low performers had time and the opportunity to improve. Many did. If they didn't, they were removed from the business," he says.

As the reduction-in-force moved forward, Trujillo became point person for internal communications, explaining how becoming leaner and more efficient would benefit customers and make Telstra stronger. "It was difficult. It was gut-wrenching. But I was heartened by the number of employees who told me the change was long overdue. It was like a breath of fresh air," he recalls. "Morale, measured by third-party surveys, actually went up…dramatically," he added.

Another major change involved a fundamental shift in corporate focus away from Canberra (the seat of government power in Australia) and toward the needs of consumers. "Government still wanted to tell us what to do," recalls Trujillo. "However, the Board took a different view that I also shared: we work for customers and shareholders – and to make Telstra a great place to work."

The workplace transformation also meant making the company more inclusive through increased cultural diversity, even as Trujillo's Australian detractors unfortunately resorted to demeaning and unrelenting public snipes at his Hispanic ancestry. "The day my appointment was announced, there was a caricature in a newspaper, labeled *New Telstra Chief*. It showed a Mexican with a serape and a sombrero, sitting on a burro with that forlorn, tired, lazy look."

Sadly, it was no isolated incident. Similar slights occurred throughout Trujillo's four-year tenure at Telstra, even though Trujillo was born and raised in Wyoming, where his family roots go back generations. When he brought in three American executives to help implement the transformation to the New Telstra, critics glibly labeled the trio The Three Amigos.

"My personal reaction was, 'how disgusting and disappointing,'" Trujillo says. "But as CEO, my job is to solve problems, not exacerbate them." Instead of focusing on the slurs, Trujillo chalked them up to Australia's relative unfamiliarity with Hispanics, its geographic isolation, and the influence of an insular press where too many reporters have limited worldviews. The experience also strengthened Trujillo's conviction that the company would be stronger if it made a concerted effort to open management doors to a broader array of employees.

"Some people like to think of diversity in terms of affirmative action. But that's a subset," says Trujillo. "Diversity is really a strategy that makes [you] stronger and more competitive by taking advantage of the strengths, perspectives, and potential of everyone in the society. You want to let people in the door to compete, regardless of their ethnicity, country of origin, what school they went to, what size, height, and weight they are. You let everybody in; then you get on the field and see who can play the best."

Trujillo himself recalls that, when he was graduating from the University of Wyoming during the early 1970s, "The company that gave me my first job tended not to hire people like me with funny last names. But that year they signed a consent decree saying they would open up their hiring process. I got hired, and I eventually I became CEO and chairman of one of the Baby Bells. If I hadn't gotten in the door, I could never have achieved what I did. This is how an opportunity society works."

During one speech to executives early in his tenure at

Telstra, Trujillo surprised the gathering by mentioning the importance of having more women in management positions, explaining that diversity is not just fair, it is also good business. "The consumer industry learned that lesson during the 1970s and 1980s," he says. "When 70 percent of all purchase decisions in the home are made by women, doesn't it make sense to have women in senior decision-making positions in the company? In fact, that's why consumer products companies that include women in senior ranks consistently experience significant growth compared to peers that do not."

Throughout his time Down Under, Trujillo was a controversial figure as many in the media and the government bristled at his highly-focused pro-customer, pro-competition, pro-investment, and pro-shareholder American management style and his visionary plan for Telstra and the media-comms industry. But he left the Aussies with a fully integrated media-comms generating world-leading results – and a dazzling mobile Internet available to virtually all Australians. And, to the extent that perception generates change one example at a time, Trujillo himself provided the best example to debunk the insidious stereotypes by which he had been described.

The Telstra story added an important chapter to the sea change in corporate perception of diversity, which is now understood less in terms of volunteered or enforced altruism and much more in terms of sound business policy and enlightened self-interest. "At heart, it's the idea of allowing everybody within a company to have the opportunity to be whatever they aspire to be. Some people aspire to be CEO; some want to be the best possible engineer or the best product manager. I want 100 percent of my people giving me 100 percent all of the time," Trujillo says. "And that can only happen if everybody has a realistic chance to reach for their dreams."

SECTION TWO

The Era of Accountability
Business as Unusual

Anybody who boards commercial airplanes knows that sinking feeling inside a crowded jetliner when something unusual happens and the pilot says...nothing.

If the plane starts bouncing around in turbulence...or the engines make funny sounds...or you descend to the runway only to zoom back up into the sky, you feel the tension rise as uninformed passengers speculate on what the problem might be. But whatever the situation is, everyone instinctively imagines something far worse.

Up in the sealed-off cockpit, of course, the flight crew knows what's happening. They're using all their skills to guide the plane safely through the flight. Unfortunately, by the time the problem is solved and the plane lands, there are 120 angry, confused ambassadors of *bad will* just itching to relay their awful experience to anyone who will listen, including *The Associated Press*.

When the financial crisis broke on Wall Street in late 2008 and early 2009, most (not all, but most) leaders of major financial firms behaved exactly like pilots sealed off in steel and glass cockpits, says John Lovallo, President of Lovallo Communications Group, an investor and financial communications firm.

Having started his career as an investment manager for several Wall Street firms, Lovallo is dismayed but not particularly surprised by that response.

"They had a real opportunity to first acknowledge the depth of the problem and then quickly come back and communicate, explicitly, how they were going to formulate and implement policies, processes, and practices that were not only going to restore trust and brand loyalty but also strengthen the business over the long term," Lovallo says. Instead, they relied on what had always worked during past times of turmoil – staying out of sight until the storm passed and self-restoring their credibility by turning profits.

"I don't think it's that easy anymore in this new era of communications and activism as stakeholders want to see the character of a corporation validated by its leadership," Lovallo says.

This time, it wasn't just investors or depositors on the hook for poor decisions made by the banks and investment houses. Taxpayer bailouts created a whole new class – a massive public class – of passengers on that plane. But no matter: except for a few token appearances, most of the CEOs stayed mum as public wrath grew.

"Take Citigroup, for example," says Lovallo. "Here's a bank that's teetering on the edge, losing massive sums of money, losing credibility with all stakeholders from the retail banking customer to the powers of Washington. But they basically said,

'Everything's under control, we're doing the right thing, just trust us.'"

Alas, the specifics were few and far between. "They never changed the broken culture," says Lovallo. "They weren't really transparent nor did they deliver a definitive plan. And I don't think they'll ever have the chance to fully rebuild trust."

Now think of the last time you were on a plane and something unusual happened and the pilot *did* talk to you. He got on the intercom right away and told you exactly what he knew. Then, for as long as the event lasted, he updated you every few minutes. Your worries didn't go away entirely, but you felt a thousand times better simply because, as the old saying goes, "information is power." And some information is better than complete impotence. Silence breeds discontent. Your audience will tolerate problems and even mistakes, but they will not tolerate arrogance. And silence is arrogance with the volume turned down.

It's the special knowledge of the pilot that allows him to tell you not just what the problem was, but, just as important, what it *wasn't*. His calming voice assures you why, specifically, the plane can withstand these conditions. Translation: *we aren't going to crash.*

Financial institutions might have used such special knowledge of their own to calm the worst public speculations post-collapse, Lovallo says. "You need to be able to take control of your own story and define it under your terms, because you're the only people who really know what's going on." Your silence only means that someone else will control the narrative. And once that narrative has been written, it is difficult, if not impossible, to change.

"If you let misinformation dominate the marketplace, then shame on you."

Rule No. 6
Trust is Profitable
Make Money the Old Fashioned Way

A banker might shrug off the latest round of criticism by consumer rights advocates as just more predictably ideological palaver.

But, when Catherine A. Allen uses blunt words for the industry, it's time to take notice. "Financial services companies have lost the trust of their customers," she says. "It didn't just happen with this crisis, but the crisis exacerbated it. If you look at statistics on consumer trust, the latest polls say that bankers are at the bottom of the pile."

Allen doesn't hate the banking industry; she's an integral part of it. In 2007, the year that *U.S. Banker* magazine honored her with a lifetime achievement award, she stepped down as founding CEO of BITS, a financial services industry consortium. Today, she's head of the Santa Fe Group, a consultancy serving leaders in the industry.

"The trouble isn't just the impact they've had on the economy, but also the fees and the usurious interest rates and the way they have treated customers over the past two to three decades," she says. "It starts at the top. CEOs must lead by example. I've even encouraged them to apologize to their customers and say, 'Look, we're sorry we got you into this mess or contributed to it, and we're going to help you out of it by giving you the best advice we can.'"

Allen, who descends from generations of bankers, can't help contrasting the current situation with the way her father carried himself as a small town bank president in the farming community of Perry, Mo., during the 1950s and 1960s.

A banker in a place like Perry (population 800) was an integral part of the community. He had to be acutely aware of its rhythms and the needs of its residents. "The banks would loan to the farmers, and the farmers would buy the grain from the grain store. When the crops came, [we] would help the farmers find markets for them, and the farmers would pay off the bank loans, and shop in the local stores. It was a community relationship. You had to have trust with your customers."

Allen's father understood implicitly that the financial well-being of his depositors wasn't just good for his own business but was his implicit social responsibility. "He gave financial advice and trained people about how to use credit or not use credit. He would tell people when they were overextending themselves."

On Sundays, farmers would often gather in the Allen family living room. "They'd talk about loans for feed or what land they might buy. He was very accessible, very involved in the community," Allen recalls. "I grew up thinking that that's what banks were about. They were there to help people, help their customers, and help the community grow. All that, in turn, helped the bank to make its profit."

Allen is too wise to try and resurrect a Norman Rockwell idyll in 21st-century America. She's the first to point out that the CEO of a multinational bank can hardly invite a million depositors over for lemonade or to get to know more than a handful of customers.

But the same principles apply then, as now, she believes. "Technology…can enable you to reestablish that kind of a relationship," she says. "By that, I mean the ability to email or respond to email; the ability to use video or webinars to reach larger groups." The profusion of data available can help banks understand their clients better than ever before, not just as profit generators, but as people working hard to get by in difficult times.

"There's no reason you couldn't Twitter people to let them know they're in danger of an overdraft. Not only do banks *not* alert their customers, but they want them to go over to be able to charge fees," Allen says. "Banks, for the most part, are doing the exact wrong thing right now by raising fees and making customers angry at a time when they're stretched."

The correct course lies in a future informed by the past. "They need to say, not in a false way, 'Here's what we want to do to help you manage your finances and keep your home. Here's what we're going to do to build a relationship.'"

As a member of such organizations as the National Foundation for Credit Counseling and the Financial Regulatory Reform Collaborative, Allen will likely provide an important voice in whatever regulatory reforms emerge from the current crisis. What she's really hoping, though, is that the banking industry reforms itself by voluntarily changing course.

That process can only commence with the recognition that a new golden age of customer satisfaction will serve everyone's interest.

— RULE No. 7 —
VALUE CAN'T BE QUANTIFIED ENTIRELY ON THE BOTTOM LINE
Make Money the Old Fashioned Way

A decade or two ago, it was relatively easy for CEOs to marginalize "socially responsible" or "sustainable" investors as well-meaning minority stockholders whose interests were unrelated to, or even in conflict with, the company's financial health and profits. After all, building long-term shareholder value is a CEO's primary task, and most investors have traditionally been interested in rising share prices and healthy dividends. A company's stance on environmental issues or labor practices seemed far from a priority consideration for many companies.

That's all changed. "Today, you ignore such investors at your peril," says Timothy Smith, Senior Vice President of the Environment, Social and Governance Group at Walden Asset Management in Boston. Today, Sustainable or Socially Responsible Investing (SRI) now accounts for roughly one of every 10 dollars invested in the United States. These investors, who insist that "value" can't be quantified entirely on a financial bottom line, are as likely to judge you as much on your environmental record or how well your suppliers in developing nations treat their workers as they are on market share expansion. But that doesn't mean they are oblivious to your financial performance or to the health of their own investments. "In the past, there was a perception that they didn't have a central interest in the bottom line. Clearly that's not true today," Smith says.

As past chairman of the Social Investment Forum in Washington, D.C., Smith is one of the leaders of a movement that major investment companies in the United States now increasingly take very seriously. Socially responsible investors are as varied as the causes they represent. One, for religious reasons, avoids companies producing alcoholic beverages or movies deemed inappropriate. Another seeks out companies that have positive environmental footprints. Yet another investor makes decisions taking into account a company's labor practices at home or overseas.

The wide variety of causes and agendas is difficult to track, and it may not always be easy to balance their concerns with those of the great mass of other shareholders. That said, the SRI phenomenon is a potential concrete business benefit for corporations savvy enough to tap that source, for at least two reasons.

First, SRI or Sustainable investors are no longer interested in just scoring social or environmental points. There's a growing recognition by both such investors and companies that responsible environmental stewardship and good corporate citizenship directly impact the bottom line. Repeated studies have shown that "socially responsible" stocks and funds perform as well, or better, than their more traditional counterparts.

Second, because of the very nature of their concerns, these investors represent an early warning system on issues they care about – providing vigilant companies with the chance to fix potential problems before they mushroom into public relations disasters. A large retailer of clothing, even one with a stated policy of buying only from suppliers with good records of fairly treating indigenous workers, may have trouble monitoring every supplier in every country. A shareholder who advocates for workers' rights could alert that company to patterns of abuse. Would you rather face a shareholder raising the issue in the relative privacy of a conference call or a television expose or viral blog excoriating the company for failing to live up to its own policies?

There are many ways to tap these shareholders. Intel, for one, is often singled out as a particularly responsive company because of its full-time Corporate Social Responsibility team. The team operates a blog dedicated to "putting social responsibility on the agenda." Company officials highlight their own social initiatives through regular postings by employees and officers, including chairman Craig Barrett, and invite public comments as well. In addition, members of the team travel throughout the country meeting with shareholder groups specifically to discuss the company's evolving global citizenship.

"They don't just come in and give a PR or traditional investor relations presentation," says Smith. "They ask what agenda items you'd like to cover in the dialogue. It's an interactive experience."

Other companies rely on more traditional methods such as conference calls or by seriously responding to shareholder resolutions at the annual meeting. "Management doesn't have to agree with everything investors say, but it's very important to be paying attention. You can't ignore these issues and let them creep up on you unaware," Smith says. "A company that automatically treats shareholder suggestions or resolutions as hostile is dangerously self-deluded."

--------------------- RULE No. 8 ---------------------

EXERCISE GOOD FAITH MANAGEMENT

Violations of Your Trust Are Acceptable Costs of Doing Business

Placing trust in another human being is never easy and always entails risk. You may get burned from time to time. But goodwill engendered through countless small gestures of trust towards your employees helps build a "trust bank" that can prevent or minimize crises, as well as encourage productivity during peace time.

Hiring an employee is the same thing as saying, "We trust you." After all, they will be handling your products, interacting with your customers, or providing critical support. They will help tell your company's story to the world every day for as long as they work for you. You believe they have integrity or you wouldn't have made them a part of the family.

Unfortunately, many companies begin undermining that trust on the new employee's first day. Someone hands them a ream of legal forms to sign along with a fat wad of rules and regulations governing everything from how much money they can spend on lunch while traveling to how many days per year they are allowed to get sick.

Now the message is precisely the opposite of the one you

sent when you hired them: "We *don't* trust you."

There's no question that companies need strong rules for the safety of customers and employees, to protect the brand, and to conform to an ever growing list of government regulations. But, as the founder and CEO of Flight Options and several other successful aviation companies, Kenn Ricci has spent much of his career drawing distinctions between necessary rules and others he believes generate unhealthy suspicion and mistrust, ultimately doing a company far more harm than good.

"We have been ingrained not to trust anything or anybody," says Ricci, who is author of the book *Management by Trust.* "We're told to be tough, to be enforcers. But the best employees, the ones who really understand your mission and can help your company be great, want to be respected, appreciated, and trusted. Creating that sort of environment requires removing barriers to trust.

"Managers set the expectations," he adds. "If you put me in an environment where you don't trust me to go to the bathroom without permission, I won't feel trusted to do anything…I won't be a productive employee."

Take the pre-set meal allowance, a standard feature at companies trying to hold the line on expenses. In Ricci's industry, pilots are always traveling, so meals are an especially significant cost. But Ricci, himself an experienced pilot, chafed at being entrusted with a multimillion-dollar jet – not to mention the lives of everyone on board – only to be told he wasn't responsible enough to order meals unsupervised. In Ricci's experience, such rules:

- Create a climate of suspicion by assuming all employees are dishonest.
- Challenge your smartest workers to figure ways to get around the rules (instead of using that creativity to help make the company better).
- Focus on your marginal employees instead of your best.

When he eliminated the meal allowance at Flight Options, did pilots suddenly order twin lobster tails at every stop? Precisely the opposite occurred. "Most pilots at the end of a long day just want a good, hot meal that reminds them of where they really want to be: home," Ricci says. With no incentive to "game the system," most pilots became custodians of this trust and *self-limited* their meal expenses. In other words, they answered trust with trust.

Encouraged, Ricci did away with other practices such as monitoring access to office supplies by clerical workers and limiting personal use of company phones. In each case, employees rose to the trust that was offered. Now that they essentially "owned" the items in the supply closet, they became protective. Stealing a box of pens from your fellow employees is suddenly different from filching from a hostile employer.

Acts of faith will inevitably be abused by some employees. That's part of the cost of trust, Ricci says. It's a cost of doing business – better business.

Even abuse itself can be cost-effective in the long-run. Say a pilot has a truly lousy day: challenging weather, flight delays, and a bum assignment. "He's unhappy with the company and with life. So he goes to the best restaurant he can find and orders the most expensive thing on the menu. And two desserts," Ricci says.

"By the time he's back at the hotel, he's no longer mad at the company. If anything, he's feeling a little contrite," says Ricci. A meal limit would have been just one more insult to add to this employee's frustration and resentment. "Instead, he's worked out his anger, solved the problem himself, and it cost you, what? An extra $20?"

An employee who consistently abuses trust is actually communicating deeper problems, Ricci says. "He's telling you he doesn't like his job." So you don't have to spend all kinds of time and money on performance reviews because he's already telling you what you need to know. It is then all the easier to identify and remove employees who are working against your mission.

Ricci, who now heads an aviation investment firm called Directional Aviation Capital, makes it clear in his book that creating a trusting environment is no easy task. "It can't just be one [little fix] in one little area," he says. "It has to start with who you hire." And, it requires your total commitment, including an acceptance of the reality that you may be abused from time to time.

Make that commitment and you will find that, in place of a workforce just doing what it's told, you've created a dynamic staff of individuals grateful for your trust and ready to sacrifice to make your company great. They will serve as ambassadors for your brand when times are good. And, when a crisis strikes, their loyalty can help give you the time you need to recover. They will stand by you because you have earned their trust.

––––––––––– **RULE NO. 9** –––––––––––

RUN TO THE LIGHT

Take Control of Stories
That Threaten Your Existence

In a very real sense, Heartland Payment Systems was no more to blame for the crisis it faced in January 2009 than a well-protected homeowner is at fault when burglars break in and steal the family heirlooms. Princeton, N.J.-based Heartland is one of the nation's largest processors of debit and credit card payments on behalf of banks and other financial institutions. Sophisticated hackers infiltrating Heartland's computers had compromised millions of card numbers, resulting in what was quickly recognized as the largest data breach in history.

It was a bet-the-company crisis for Heartland, as its reputation and livelihood depend on its safely and securely processing millions of sensitive transactions. To make matters worse, the crisis unfolded just as the nation's banking system was sinking into the worst financial crisis in generations. "My immediate assessment was that this could put the company out of business," recalls Chief Executive Robert Carr.

Some of the company's response decisions were immediate and unquestioned. In particular, Heartland fully informed its board of directors, as well as law enforcement agencies such as the FBI and the Secret Service. It would also, obviously, have to contact the various card brands with which Heartland works.

Beyond these initial steps, the choices were far less clear. Other companies facing data breaches had chosen a deliberately low-key approach, informing just those necessary parties and releasing as little public information as possible. As the stakes grew ever greater, the question loomed: should the company go public with the news or remain quiet about it? Protocol demanded silence for at least a few days while Heartland waited to hear from law enforcement officials if a public announcement would disrupt current investigations. Inside and outside computer forensics experts also needed time to determine the actual scope of the problem.

As the victim of a crime and certainly not the perpetrator, would not the company be justified in quietly working with law enforcement and key clients to solve the matter as unobtrusively as possible? A public announcement might also bring an avalanche of negative publicity, throwing more fuel on the fire.

"There's no outright obligation necessarily," Carr says. "Certainly, it's not easy to know whether or not public disclosure is required." At the same time, if Heartland was a crime victim,

Carr knew that playing the victim was *not* going to restore the company's reputation. Heartland's customers didn't need another victim; they needed a bold leader responding decisively and backing up its assurances with action.

Advised by the government that an announcement would not, in fact, interfere with investigations, and aware by now of the full scope of the disaster, Carr settled on a strategy of maximum openness and communication, beginning with a full public announcement. Doing so meant overruling the more cautious voices on the company's management team who were arguing vehemently against going public. "I pulled rank. I don't do that very often but I said, 'We're going to do it,' and we did."

It was a decision that ultimately kept a bad situation from becoming infinitely worse, as Carr galvanized the workforce in a successful effort to save the company and reassure clients that their well-being was top priority. Within a few weeks, news reports in the business media were spending as much, if not more, time on Heartland's successful response as on the life-threatening crisis itself.

As Carr deconstructs the experience, he insists the response only amounted to doing "the logical thing." One of Carr's earliest concerns was for the legal protection of employees. Because the immediate response required working with employees to identify and analyze the breach, Carr feared that workers who sold Heartland stock, even independently of any knowledge of the situation, might be exposed to insider trading allegations. "I was concerned that they would sell their stock, and so, with all of the publicity about insider trading with Martha Stewart and all that, I didn't want to expose our employees to that accusation, even if it wasn't true, even if they didn't know." Solution: by making the announcement via the Internet and other media *before* trading opened after the scandal, Carr provided a strong measure of protection for his workers.

Going public also allowed Heartland to:

Reassure clients. On the same morning the announcement went public, Carr made an internal call to all company employees. After explaining the situation, he asked employees to immediately begin visiting more than 150,000 customers who process cards using Heartland technology, to explain what was going on, to reassure them that none of their own business information had been compromised, and to explain what Heartland was doing to solve the problem.

"It was clear that our competitors were going to try to use this to take our customers away from us," Carr says. "I felt that, if we were in the door first, being up front and open about it, our customers would appreciate that. We are the company that started the Merchant Bill of Rights, and we talk about transparency and full disclosure and integrity and being honest with our customers. If they learned about this [crisis] from somebody else, I thought that would be a disaster for us."

Enlist the workforce. Carr's words to employees were frank and honest. "I said we don't know how bad this is going to be. We know our competitors are going to try to take advantage of this situation, and we all need to pull together and work harder than we've ever worked to get our message out and to give the best possible service that we've ever given to our customers." Carr was thus fully empowering Heartland employees to act as part of the solution by taking focused and productive steps.

"I believe our employees felt proud that we were taking the position we took and felt like they were part of a team that was on a mission," Carr recalls. "We were the victims of a crime, we weren't the criminals. It felt like the company rallied together as we never had before. I think it has made us stronger."

Control the story. Companies that try to keep quiet about a crisis usually find themselves playing defense when word finally gets out. Because they've been hiding, all of their statements become suspect, even when they are refuting false reports.

By contrast, Heartland's forward and open strategy enabled the company to take control of the story. By establishing themselves as the primary narrators of what the crisis *was*, they were able to credibly explain what the crisis *was not*. The message – that the breach was a serious one but was well contained within practicable limits – was altogether credible as a result. This theme became the story, allowing Heartland, in effect, to control the narrative.

"We basically said that no Social Security numbers were compromised, no addresses, no email addresses. The card numbers were stolen. So, it's not identity theft. It's the theft of a card number," Carr says.

Pioneer industry-wide solutions. Given the highly competitive nature of its industry, Heartland might have kept its knowledge of the hackers and their methods close to its vest. After all, a similar problem for a competitor might mean more business for Heartland. On the belief that hackers threaten the entire industry, not to mention consumers, Carr did the opposite. "We went to our competitors and handed out the 'malware,' the software that was used for our breach, and we educated them about everything that we could."

In the wake of the crisis, Heartland quickly developed a proprietary encryption system that scrambles numbers from the moment they're swiped in a store, thus preventing hackers from reading them. Heartland made this technology available to anyone who wanted it, even as the company took the lead in forming a group called Payment Processors Information Sharing Council. The organization works with law enforcement on ways to combat cybercrime.

These and other steps brought Heartland safely back from the brink of disaster. Company stock, which plummeted from $15.18 to $3.43 per share, began a recovery to nearly $15 per share by early fall of 2009. The headline in a *Computerworld* magazine read, "Heartland Commended for Breach Response." *BusinessWeek*, meanwhile, weighed in on "what other companies can learn" from Heartland's bold response.

Most important, Heartland, through the swift and decisive leadership of its CEO, had converted a terrible dilemma into an opportunity to further brand itself as a leader committed to prevention, industry-wide solutions, honest communication, and putting customers and employees first.

SECTION THREE

THE NEED FOR A
CRISIS CULTURE
Seeing the World Differently Now and in the Future

What are your crisis plans? If you cannot at least begin a thorough, logical, and orderly response to that question, you're in trouble already. To succeed these days, all companies need to operate in a crisis culture and live in a state of nonstop readiness for the next unexpected event.

It's important to qualify what we mean, and don't mean, by "crisis culture." It does not mean that you and your employees live in constant dread. A crisis is emphatically not the same as a *fear culture*.

Quite to the contrary, a climate of fear is just what may result in the absence of a crisis culture. Fear, after all, stems mainly from the unknown. When emergencies arise and people lack a basic plan of how to respond, how to communicate internally and externally, and what the next step might be, they have no choice but to make it up as they go along. That's when panic sets in.

By contrast, a crisis culture is one in which everyone knows what he or she is supposed to do in an emergency before it happens. Compare it to working out. You wouldn't set out on a two-mile swim across a channel without having first done some serious laps at the Y over a period of time. So why put yourself in a position of figuring out how to respond to a crisis at the very moment you're trying to respond to it?

Just like exercise, crisis preparation makes you healthier even if you never face that crisis at all. There's a fine line between crisis and change. A company ready for crisis is a company ready for change. A company riding along on cruise control without considering the possibility of crisis may be missing opportunities for positive change. You will not know the exact specifics of the crisis until it happens, nor can you know for sure when it will happen. But with a chain of communication and response in place, you and your colleagues will know how to adapt calmly, decisively, and flexibly to most any situation.

RULE No. 10

TURF WAR IS A HUMAN INSTINCT

How Corporate Silos Can Be More Dangerous Than Missile Silos

As the chief executive of Global Rescue, Daniel Richards is never surprised when he hears from a company that needs help rescuing employees stuck in a foreign battle zone. As his company name makes clear, helping people out of serious, often life-threatening jams is what they do best.

What *does* surprise Richards, time after time, is how many companies face perilous situations totally unprepared even though they're the ones who sent the employees into a troubled area to begin with. "Those are the 2 a.m. phone calls that come into our operations center from a company with 10 people in Lebanon as the Hezbollah-Israeli conflict is starting, and they've got no idea what to do. We've actually had that happen," Richards says.

Chaos and panic are two of the expected results of such unpreparedness. Even more insidious is when different departments in a company form silos to protect their own interests. "When it comes time to actually mobilize a response, different departments in the company can even act in an obstructionist way, interfering with people trying to solve the crisis," Richards says.

Such obstructionism is extremely destructive under any circumstance and all the more tragic when lives are at risk. The bottom line is that you cannot assume that your teams will do the right thing (even when they are well-meaning), especially when the right thing calls for change. Crisis response is not about self-preservation, but about team preservation. It requires a coordinated effort to save the most critical things first, regardless of territory. If people fight turf wars when lives are in jeopardy, imagine how much more fiercely self-interested their behavior in non-life-threatening crises will be.

"We had a Fortune 25 company call us and retain us to go get their people. The way they approached retaining us, from the beginning, was not dissimilar from the way they'd approach retaining a company that supplied nuts and bolts. Purchasing was involved, and procurement, and legal, and everybody wanted something," he says. "Finally…a C-level individual had to assert himself in order to get through all of the crippling bureaucracy that was going to prevent us from doing the things that needed to be done. We've seen that over and over. Sometimes these organizations get out of their own way and let the problem be solved, and sometimes they don't."

While not all situations are so life-critical, more commonplace crises can be just as debilitating. As Richards says, "All you have to do is pick up the paper to see that a lot of companies aren't prepared for financial crises either."

Too often, companies go through elaborate motions by preparing an exhaustively detailed crisis preparation plan, only to file the plan away and return to business as usual. "There's a very big market today for crisis consultants, disaster preparedness, redundancy of systems, and other things," Richards says. The real test comes in putting the plan to use during an actual event. If only one or two people in your company remember the contents of the plan, that's as good as having no plan at all.

To make the plan viable, you'll need an ongoing crisis team that actively and regularly trains for a variety of emergency situations. "The saying is that generals are always fighting the last war," Richards says. "Well, people are always preparing for what they have experience with, and that typically is the last crisis they faced. The problem is that, as the nature of the future crisis changes or the amplitude or magnitude changes, you may not be prepared."

As such, training should include specific scenarios (a natural disaster, an accounting crisis, a mishap involving your products and customers, etc.) but should be general enough so that the lessons can be transferred from one type of crisis to the next. And all scenarios, regardless of specifics, should include the assumption that digital media can, and will, take the story viral at any moment. In the end, what you are trying to achieve is a sense of teamwork and togetherness that allows you to meet and overcome exigent circumstances. You are trying to build trust and an instinct for the overall mission rather than self-preservation. That's why it is your responsibility to make clear to everyone exactly what you mean by teamwork.

By so doing, you also communicate to your staff that you are prepared, savvy, and committed to protecting them and the company. You will be rewarded with increased loyalty, Richards says. "When it comes to morale in the organization, if you're not going to respond and support your people, it becomes very difficult to lead and motivate."

— Rule No. 11 —
Everyone Must Sacrifice, You Go First
Buy Your Wastebasket at Staples

Most people know the score. Employees, investors, and the public understand that economies rise and fall and they expect companies to have good years and bad.

They will grant more latitude than you might expect to companies struggling with financial challenges, provided that top managers are open and honest with the numbers and are willing to share in the sacrifice.

But they will never understand or forgive corporate executives who prosper or appear to prosper while the balance sheet bleeds red, the stock price tumbles, and the company takes bailout money from taxpayers.

Consider John Thain, one of the more brilliant financial minds of our time. The son of a small town doctor in the Midwest, Thain enrolled at MIT with plans to become an engineer. He turned instead to Wall Street, where hard work and innovative decisions hoisted him up the ladder at Goldman Sachs and on to the top spot at the New York Stock Exchange.

His appointment in late 2007 to lead Merrill Lynch out of the financial mess left by previous Merrill CEO Stan O'Neal was almost universally hailed as a major step toward a turnaround.

And then came the $1,400 wastebasket.

When it surfaced that Thain, hired specifically to bring financial discipline to the ailing brokerage, had spent $1.22 million of company money to decorate his office, critics of Corporate Greed went into overdrive. The tab included $87,000 for an area rug, $68,000 for an antique credenza, and $25,000 for a pedestal table. But nothing quite hit home like that wastebasket. Thain quickly apologized and refunded the company for the entire renovation out of his own pocket. Unfortunately, the damage was done.

Later, when reports surfaced that Thain had approved sizable bonuses to his executives (though not to himself) just before a distressed Merrill was sold to Bank of America, the public didn't need to hear specifics in order pass judgment. They had already heard all the specifics they needed.

Thain did not cause the financial catastrophe that brought down Merrill Lynch, but the saga will most likely follow him for the rest of his life. Why? Because a man who'd even consider buying a $1,400 wastebasket cannot by definition be a man capable of *sharing in sacrifice.*

Sadly, Thain's story is hardly unique. This financial crisis has abounded in tales of executives flying private jets to beg for bailouts, partying at exclusive spas, or reaping bonuses while shareholders suffer. In virtually every case, the amount of money involved is negligible compared with the symbolism and the damage to the reputations of the individuals and companies involved.

Less well-known, and too few in number, are stories such as that of Boston's Beth Israel Deaconess Medical Center and its CEO Paul Levy.

In early 2009, the downward economy left the Beth Israel Deaconess, a legendary Harvard teaching hospital, with a $20 million budget gap and the prospective layoff of 600 of its 6,300 employees. They were mainly lower-paid workers in food services, transportation, and other departments.

At many companies, the CEO might have squirreled away in a conference room with the CFO and a few other top executives, crunching numbers and preparing the layoff announcement. Determined to save as many jobs as possible, Levy took the opposite approach. First, he sent out mass emails to employees offering full, clear details on the problems the hospital faced.

Every employee, at every level, was given full access to the numbers. Levy subsequently posted the figures on his blog, "Running a Hospital" (see Rule #29 – The Social Media is the CEO's 21st Century Telephone).

Why such candor? Levy explains, "To me, it is so commonsensical. People need to understand the dimensions of the problem to help solve the problem. If you're going to ask them for advice and actions, they have to know the real story."

Once all the numbers were on the table, Levy turned to the employees and asked if they'd be willing to accept lower pay in return for saving the jobs of their co-workers. Crucially, Levy and other top managers led the way by taking voluntary cuts in their own pay. "Absent that, people would have felt they were being taken advantage of, that they were saps," Levy says. "If you're asking people to make sacrifices, and they think you're not doing the same, then they're going to say, 'Well, there goes top management again, taking advantage of us.'"

The response, from celebrated physicians and department heads on down to clerical and maintenance workers, was overwhelming. Employees took pay cuts, accepted a freeze on

401(k) contributions, scaled back vacation days, and returned recent raises. Many employees dug into their personal bank accounts and mailed checks. "I wasn't surprised by the nature of their response," Levy says. "But I was surprised by the intensity. It was very, very sweet."

Most of the 600 jobs were saved. As an ancillary (but hardly inconsiderable) benefit, the story generated positive publicity and goodwill for the hospital and for Levy himself. A CBS News report captured the sentiment: "The staff at Beth Israel Deaconess Medical Center in Boston made its name by caring for its patients," the segment began, "but these days, they're caring for each other."

Now that the hospital has overcome its financial troubles, one lesson seems inescapably clear: let your constituents suffer alone and you may carry a black mark forever. Take the lead in sacrificing, and they'll follow you proudly.

——————— Rule No. 12 ———————

If You Really Want to Gain, Lose Something First

Give the Guy Your Gun

Stratford Sherman walked into his first meeting with Jack Welch braced for battle. As a young editor with *Fortune* magazine, Sherman had been assigned to interview General Electric's legendarily hard-nosed CEO at a time (1986) when GE was embroiled in an embarrassing crisis. The investment firm Kidder Peabody, which GE had recently purchased, was implicated in insider trading. Although the suspect trades took place prior to the acquisition, the scandal threatened GE's (and Welch's) reputation for competence and integrity.

Based on nearly a decade interviewing CEOs in similar circumstances, Sherman thought he knew what to expect from Welch, whom he'd never met: Welch would evade the tough questions, try to spin the story in his favor, and, when pressed, become defensive.

Imagine Sherman's surprise when Welch started the interview by saying, "We screwed up. We didn't do our due diligence. That's totally our fault."

Welch frankly acknowledged Kidder's guilt, detailed what GE knew about the situation, and talked about how the company planned to cooperate with New York's then-District Attorney Rudy Giuliani.

"He said all of this within the first seven minutes of our initial conversation," Sherman recalls. "I had never, *ever* had a chief executive open a conversation by saying he was wrong. Those words just never passed the lips of most CEOs."

What Sherman didn't realize at the time but would later fully appreciate was that Welch had expertly employed one of the most valuable and under-utilized tools of leadership: giving the other guy your gun.

Clint Eastwood may have become the stuff of legend when he cocked a .44 magnum and hissed, "Go ahead, make my day!" Alas, such fantasies express the constant seething emotions just under the surface of polite society. But they do not define true strength and leadership, especially under duress. Quite to the contrary, the real test of leaders is in their capacity to actually un-cock their weapons when it is strategically wise to do so.

To be sure, we are not talking about surrendering out of fear or compromising personal and institutional values or interests. We are talking instead about important concessions to potential adversaries that disarm their arsenals, build trust, and set the stage for mutual gain. To be effective, however, strategic concessions should be made *at the outset of the relationship, before the other person demands them.*

"This is not about weakness or giving in. It's about a different method for reaching a better outcome," says Sherman, now a best-selling business author and partner in Accompli, an advisory firm that serves senior leaders of large-scale change.

By freely offering Sherman a story that the journalist wanted to pry loose (in other words, by giving Sherman his gun), Welch yielded a little but gained much more by winning the trust and admiration of a professional who, over time, would become an important ally. In 1993, Sherman co-authored the bestselling *Control Your Destiny or Someone Else Will*, a positive analysis of the Welch years at GE. The book, now in its fourth edition, has become a standard business text.

"In a moment, in a flash, he completely won me over," Sherman recalls. "He won my sympathy and affection. I have a lifelong affection for this guy, and it began with that revelation of honesty, that vulnerability."

He adds, "Welch knew GE had much greater interests at stake than Kidder Peabody. If he had to write off all of Kidder Peabody, that was better than letting it sink GE's reputation for integrity. There was very clear-minded thinking underlying all of this. It wasn't in any way weak."

Sherman has found the same approach highly useful in his own career. As a journalist, he learned to begin interviews with top executives by volunteering to use any information as background knowledge, without quoting them. Most CEOs are leery of interviews precisely because anything they say is bound to appear in print, especially if it is sensitive, provocative, or embarrassing. "My willingness to go off the record, in effect, handed them my gun. It eliminated my power over them and maximized their power over me, which made them comfortable.

Feeling comfortable, they were very much inclined to talk freely.

"It enabled a relationship of trust," he adds. "Even though I couldn't use anything they said without getting their permission, what they told me was now [a part of] my awareness. That knowledge could quite ethically inform my subsequent reporting, [determining whom] I would subsequently interview and what questions to ask." And, during the course of an interview, if a comment seemed particularly pertinent, Sherman would politely ask if it they would mind going on the record for that one comment. With the ground rules thus tilted in their favor, the CEOs usually agreed, and Sherman came away with a solid quote for his story, enhanced understanding of the crucial issues, and the basis for a productive, ongoing relationship with the executive.

Even in the context of a normal business relationship, there is the potential for both sides to brandish loaded weapons at the first hint of discord. Today, as a consultant, Sherman's approach is to minimize that likelihood, offering clients success-fee arrangements that give them significant latitude in determining whether they've been sufficiently satisfied with the results to pay the bill.

"In our experience we haven't had a situation where success wasn't achieved and where the client didn't pay. I think our putting so much trust in them makes them more concerned about seeing that our interests are met, as well as theirs. They no longer see us as an adversary. We enter into a form of partnership together."

In each instance, giving the other guy your gun results in greater gain. Says Sherman, "If you do it right, you fundamentally change the nature of the relationship."

── Rule No. 13 ──
Lawyers Don't Drive the Bus
How to Avoid Tunnel Vision During Crisis

We wouldn't think of doing business without strong legal counsel, and you wouldn't, either. But you are not compelled to always *take* their advice, or accord them overriding authority within your crisis team.

"A lot of companies have their crisis management under the auspices of general counsel or outside counsel. I think that is an enormous mistake," says Steven C. Parrish, who retired in March 2008 as Senior Vice President of Corporate Affairs at Altria Group, the parent of Philip Morris. Parrish, by the way, is a lawyer who has served as both a corporate general counsel and outside counsel. "Under the code of professional responsibility you cannot, you are not *allowed* to take off your lawyer hat," he says. "You have to protect the legal interests of the company. That, by definition, appropriately requires counsel to be very conservative and cautious about what is said to the public and what is said to the employees."

While caution is thus mandated in its place, the desire to stay out of legal trouble can create a debilitating tunnel vision if it defines your crisis strategy. Says Parrish, "You can manage a crisis so that you never get sued, but [in the end] you can lose by having your reputation destroyed because there's no communication, or it's the wrong communication." A lawyerly press release or public statement is often as dangerous as no statement at all. Legal language, so vital and appropriate in the courtroom or in contract negotiations, won't help you win cases in the court of public opinion during a crisis.

Parrish cites a well-known Philip Morris case from the

mid-1990s, when chemical impurities accidentally introduced during the manufacturing process tainted Marlboro and other brands of cigarettes, causing an unpleasant taste and eye, nose, and throat irritation in some smokers. Although the problem affected only a small percentage of production and resulted in no serious injuries or deaths, Philip Morris responded quickly with a massive recall and public information campaign. The campaign ultimately succeeded in limiting the scope of the crisis, yet Parrish recalls that the crisis management team's efforts were at first impeded by lawyerly meddling.

"One of the things we did wrong during the recall [was that] we had lawyers with way too much influence over the press releases," Parrish recalls. "They were, in a couple of instances, incomprehensible." In an industry such as tobacco, where public skepticism already abounds, clear communication is vital. Parrish adds, "When people can't understand [a release], or it's obviously written by a lawyer, people don't trust what you're saying." If you don't present your statements and intentions in plain English, you invite derision from legions of confused reporters, bloggers, politicians, and pundits. Worse, you invite them to do their own translating, making serious and potentially damaging mistakes along the way.

As a crisis breaks and you're ready to go forward with a statement laying out the facts, and what you plan to do to correct the situation, by all means, show it to counsel. But be prepared for her to get out her red pen. "You can't say that," she'll warn you. "Three years from now someone's going to call that up and use it as the basis of a lawsuit." Don't get angry. It's her job to tell you that. But don't tear up that statement, either. Your job is to look her in the eye and say that without bold action, in three years you may not have a company at all.

Rule No. 14
There's Value in Being Wrong
Creating a Culture of Candor

Sycophancy is sure good for the ego. Alas, that's all it's good for. In fact, flattery and knee-jerk agreeability from staffers, senior or otherwise, minimize opportunities for corporate improvement at every level. Worse, in a crisis, when the integrity and future of the company are on the line, it's death to stifle honest feedback from everyone around you. Creating an environment of candor – however difficult it may be to do so in the short term – is the ideal alternative that can provide the early warning systems needed to master every variety of crisis under the sun.

In recent years, the importance of candor within an organization has escalated as work becomes less rote and more creative. Indeed, as a salutary and emerging force in corporate life, candor needs to be seen in a larger socio-economic context.

In past decades, when employees were seen as more or less interchangeable, popular wisdom held that the best corporate managers were those with the best systems. Because machines could manufacture products and process information faster and more accurately than any human, the primary challenge was to organize and regiment the fallible and largely interchangeable humans needed to keep the machines running.

"It was all about getting people within hierarchies to do relatively simple things more efficiently because of great systems," says Stratford Sherman, a partner with Accompli, a change advisory group serving senior corporate leaders, and co-author of the best-selling *Control Your Destiny or Someone Else Will.*

But a funny thing happened on the way to the Orwellian

future. Technology has not *enshrined* hierarchical, impersonal management systems as the holy grail of corporate process. It has *destroyed* them.

"Companies don't need so many workers and managers performing rote tasks," Sherman says. "What's left are leaner, flatter organizations with fewer people in them. As the number of players is reduced, the work they do becomes less mechanistic. Here's what we've learned: people are able to add value only to the degree that they can actually think and speak openly."

Companies that insist on strict hierarchies and prefabricated approaches to problems are just like the British commanders who sent exposed and rigidly deployed lines of Redcoats into battle against flexible and well-hidden Colonials. They are fighting the last war instead of the current one.

To migrate from the old industrial and pre-industrial systems to leadership models that can succeed in the 21st century, managers must transform their relationships with those they manage. And the key to that is fostering cultures that encourage or even mandate *candor*. "Great decisions require great information," Sherman says, "If you don't have candor and teams working together, you can't have great decisions. It's just not possible. Getting better decisions requires developing a culture of candor."

Sherman spent years studying the management methods and philosophies of Jack Welch, the legendary GE chief executive. What impressed him most was the sincere value Welch placed on the opinions of others – the more directly and freely expressed, the better.

Once per quarter, Welch would gather managers from GE's far-flung business operations for meetings of the company's corporate executive council. Specific discussions of budgets and revenues were off the table. Instead, Welch wanted to hear candid thoughts on where the future was headed and what GE needed to do, even (especially!) if those thoughts ran counter to his personal preconceptions.

"Because of the scope of GE's businesses, the folks in that room were unbelievably well informed about a lot of stuff," says Sherman. "The effect of getting them all in one room was that they made the CEO a hell of a lot smarter, but only because they were free to be candid. Welch had a very powerful and ultimately humble recognition that the brilliance that was attributed to him was due in very large part to being part of a community where candor was intensely valued."

To that end the CEO must overcome the infallibility complex – the idea that being the leader means you must by definition know more than everyone and necessarily be correct.

"Mature leaders over time become more rather than less open to the idea that they might be wrong and could improve," Sherman says. "The really great leaders aren't threatened by their own imperfections. On the contrary, they are hungry for improvement. Those are the really strong, grounded, inspiring people that other people love to follow. They're the ones who are comfortable saying, 'I was wrong' or 'I don't know.'"

Communicate impatience or sensitivity about views contradicting your own and every subordinate, from the receptionist in the lobby downstairs to your CFO, will clam up. Only you can guarantee candor.

Give people in your organization a useful glimpse into your decision making and thought processes. Sherman cites one company where the managers were becoming extremely frustrated because the CEO seemed to reverse course without warning. As a result, they were reluctant to stick their necks out with new ideas or suggestions that might be approved one minute, then summarily rejected the next.

"It turned out that this executive was getting important financial updates every two weeks," Sherman says. "So, he might say something in Week One, then make a course correction in Week Three when revised data came out." But he hadn't advised his staff accordingly, so his people thought he was simply capricious. Once they knew what was going on, they were more willing to change course with him.

To see how lack of candor makes bad situations far worse, look no farther than Merrill Lynch in 2007 under then-CEO Stan O'Neal, Sherman suggests. In October of that year, when Merrill announced a record quarterly loss of $8.4 billion related to the subprime meltdown, nobody seemed more surprised than the company itself. As the website MoneyMorning.com reported when O'Neal was fired later that month, "What really stunned Wall Street...was the fact that Merrill clearly didn't have a clue about the depth of its problems."

O'Neal, as CEO, had a reputation not just as a risk-taker, but as an aloof executive who surrounded himself with a small number of hand-picked advisors. It's hard to say to what extent, if any, these people insulated O'Neal from bad news, but, clearly, if anyone had the nerve or foresight to warn O'Neal about the dangers of the company's exposure to massive amounts of shaky mortgage securities, the message never got through. According to news coverage, O'Neal had his own problems with candor, discussing a possible merger with Wachovia without first informing the board. The Wachovia deal fell through, O'Neal was out, and a legendary company, unable to recover on its own, is now a Bank of America vassal.

Sherman contrasts Merrill and Stan O'Neal with JP Morgan and its fiery, blunt leader, Jamie Dimon, proclaimed "The Toughest Guy on Wall Street" by *Fortune* magazine. Crucially, that toughness does not entail browbeating underlings who happen to disagree with him. On the contrary, Sherman points out that Dimon intentionally surrounds himself with people tough enough to tell him when he's wrong. That internal heat helped Dimon and JP Morgan navigate the financial crisis with their finances and reputation intact.

One way to foster open environments is to simply come right out and affirm that candor is important. "Declare that it's something you are going to demand," Sherman suggests. "Move off the agenda at your next meeting and say, 'Let's spend the next hour talking about candor; what's promoting it and what's inhibiting it.'"

Note that authentic discussion does not require CEOs to be anything less than human and fallible. You will have emotional reactions and you may even get angry. The key is in being able to differentiate emotion from fact and to draw a distinct line between the two. "What usually happens is a leader gets totally frustrated and, out of that emotional state, they make some angry statement and they throw some facts in and they think they are making a factual statement. But all they're really doing is expressing anger," Sherman says.

When facts are abused to support anger, subordinates have no choice but to go along with you or face the consequences. Openness is destroyed. But getting angry shows you're only human, Sherman says. Tell your staff what made you angry. Then return to the factual discussions after everyone has calmed down. In that way, people can accommodate the human factor – they can forgive the chief executive's outburst – without ever having to sacrifice the right to openly share their thoughts and expertise.

As Sherman puts it, "Now that you've faced, not just business reality, but human reality, your company is a place where value is created by people and not by machines."

--------------------- **RULE No. 15** ---------------------

THE 24 HOUR RULE

What Your Employees Say and Do in the First Moment of a Crisis Matter Most

---

In any other context, the collapse of legendary Arthur Andersen LLC in 2002 would have been the biggest lead story of the year. Against the backdrop of catastrophic frauds perpetrated by Ken Lay and his team at Enron, however, the fate of the energy company's outside accountants was only the secondary story, however staggering in its own right.

The Andersen story simply did not have the sensationalistic elements that riveted public attention on Enron. No one suggested that Andersen was actively engaged in the kind of criminal behavior that made Enron a synonym for corruption, dishonesty, and greed.

In the end, what brought the nearly century-old accountancy to its knees was the shredding of documents *after* the crisis began to unfold.

"Enron got what it deserved, but most of Andersen's problems were probably manageable," says Ty Cobb, a Washington lawyer specializing in white collar criminal defense cases. "Had they not destroyed documents, not assisted Enron in destroying documents, they probably would still be flourishing.... What Enron did was highly irregular. What Anderson did was, for the most part, routine until the moment they decided that it was okay to purge."

All of which suggests that Andersen's problems were not related to endemic corruption and venality, but to *a serious communications and leadership gap*. Somewhere along the line, managers inadequately trained in crisis response found themselves in the position of making split-second decisions with lasting consequences for themselves and the entire company. Years later Andersen is still one of the most famous, but certainly not the only case that dramatically underscores what leaders must do to prevent carelessness in situations where it matters most.

Legions of high-profile politicians and their aides have learned the meaning of the adage, "It's not the crime, it's the cover-up." Indeed, they've learned it the hard way. Consider White House advisor Scooter Libby, convicted in 2007 for lying and obstructing justice in what ultimately proved to be a nonexistent criminal case. Cobb, partner at the D.C. law firm Hogan & Hartson and a veteran counselor to some of the highest-profile figures in the political and corporate worlds, advises that the lesson is every bit as relevant for corporations as it is for public figures.

The ways in which your managers and employees respond in the early hours of a crisis can spell the difference between a manageable event and one that could send employees to prison and irrevocably damage the corporate brand. As such, your crisis response system needs to be finely honed and adapted for communications at every level of management and in every branch and location.

"Frankly, half of [corporate] investigations, give or take 20 percent, don't go anywhere, other than a false statement charge or obstruction of justice charge based on statements that are made or documents that are destroyed in the first 24 hours," Cobb says.

In most investigations of corporate crime, first impressions are impossible to shake off. Afterwards, you and your company must live with the fallout, good or bad. All the high-priced lawyers and sophisticated public relations campaigns in the world won't be able to buy back those first 24 hours.

According to Cobb, there are two primary danger areas: lying or misleading investigators and destroying documents. Crisis preparation and crisis management demand ongoing practical training for employees at every level who might someday be in a position to talk to law enforcers or handle sensitive materials.

Say you run a manufacturing firm with factories scattered across the country. Investigators, learning of a possible crime or major infraction at one of the plants, arrive at the door bearing search warrants or subpoenas and asking questions. Meanwhile, back at headquarters, you're still trying to sort out what's going on and who the "relevant" employees actually are. At that moment, those very employees may well be making split-second decisions with lasting consequences.

Your employees "are in a position to do even more harm to the company than they already have, and that happens all the time. It happens by deleting emails, or destroying documents or persuading subordinates to lie," Cobb says.

Such bad actions usually result not from criminal intent but from confusion in the heat of the moment or even from simple embarrassment. Cobb handled one case involving a sales representative for a Maryland company who was being investigated for selling a chemical that, in addition to its legitimate manufacturing properties, is a key component of mustard gas – and she was selling it to foreign agents.

According to Cobb, the sales representative was duped by the agents posing as legitimate buyers. When U.S. Customs investigators presented a search warrant, the woman made her first mistake by speaking with them extemporaneously and without counsel. During the conversation, she sincerely denied doing business with the foreign agents.

Cobb recalls that, responding later to a subpoena, the woman came across "two or three documents that indicated that she actually had done business with that particular country." Instead of alerting officials to her mistake, she compounded the error by destroying the documents. "It was purely out of embarrassment that she had misspoken to the customs person that she did it. But the document destruction was clearly criminal," Cobb says, "and she ended up being criminally convicted."

As a result, the company itself also faced a difficult plea case with the government. "The fact that she had done this created a perception that the company did feel guilty about something, where its principle defense was that it had been duped by these other people. And that was a real defense and it was true, but the legitimacy was undermined by this stupid response."

Such incidents dramatize why corporate leaders must ensure there is an emergency response protocol focused on those crucial 24 hours, Cobb says. Inside and outside counsel must guide the process. Among the first decisions is whether, and in what way, employees speak with investigators.

On the one hand, the company is legally prohibited from telling employees not to speak with investigators, Cobb says. However, the company can advise employees that, while they have the right to speak, they are not obligated to do so and that the company can and will provide counsel.

Most important, though, "if they do talk, it's imperative that they be completely truthful and, to the extent that they misrepresent anything or misstate something, or are in error in any information they provide, that they alert in-house counsel immediately so they can be protected and a correction made," Cobb advises. "The worst thing that happens is they lie to people." That's when one small act of dishonesty becomes a crisis that shakes your company to its foundations.

Such momentous consequences often turn on processes and practices that can seem miniscule compared with the larger strategic events that preoccupy CEOs. Yet it is another instance of a central, rather daunting lesson that leaders must learn from the difficult realities that now shape modern business. The lesson is that, for leaders to be truly effective, they must be constantly rethinking their priorities, well-advised that something as "small" as a training program for middle-level managers is potentially as "big" as a decision to expand operations to a new continent.

—————— RULE No. 16 ——————

LEADERS CANNOT CHANGE HUMAN INSTINCTS

Measure and Manage the Biology of Fear

As a corporate crisis unfolds, a normally communicative, competent manager suddenly seems incapable of making a decision. "Too risky," he snaps whenever someone suggests a course of action that varies from standard practice.

Another manager focuses with laser intensity on one specific problem while ignoring the larger threats cropping up all around, or insists on approaches that soothe immediate fears but may pose greater long-term harm than good.

A universal email from the top floor, urging calm and downplaying the crisis, only intensifies the rumors and uneasiness spreading on every floor. Absent hard information, employees connect real and imaginary dots to create patterns of conspiracy and doom. Each department, meanwhile, retreats into the perceived safety of its own silo. Accounting protects its back against purchasing, which insists that the fault actually lies with those in marketing.

Any leader who has spent much time in a corporate environment knows the frustration of trying to erase counterproductive behaviors that trap people under pressure and that clearly undermine the company's best interests. Additionally frustrating is that these behaviors seem so stubbornly resistant to change. Coaching, cajoling, and reassurances all yield the same indifferent results as the very next crisis typically triggers the usual responses.

Many of us simply ascribe such repetitive fear responses to intellectual weakness or illogic, but neuroscientists are now coming up with an entirely different story. If their hypotheses are correct – and they're pretty persuasive to our laity ears – the enemy is far more imposing than individual personality deficiencies, which are still correctable albeit persistently stubborn.

Scott Huettel, Ph.D., a neuroscientist at Duke University, is part of a growing field of "neuroeconomists" who believe that what, in a modern setting, seems to be illogical responses may, in fact, result from very logical, precise brain systems designed for self-protection in an immediately dangerous world. We look at the Darwinian challenges of predatory hunting and shelter-seeking from the elements as prehistorically ancestral. In fact, a mere eye blink separates us from the ancient evolutionary struggles.

"We have evolved to respond to threats that are very personal, that are social in nature, that are well-defined, and have relatively immediate consequences," says Huettel, Director of Duke's Center for Neuroeconomic Studies. In ancient eras, "you didn't have technology. You didn't have planning for years in the future. You didn't have reasoning about abstract concepts, or people disconnected from their local communities and interacting with people they've never met.

"In the modern corporate world, the real challenges are abstract," explains Huettel. "They may not be directed at us, personally. Even so, while the sources of fear are very different from those in our evolutionary history, *the mechanisms that we have for dealing with them are essentially the same*".

For corporate leaders, such atavisms are of more than theoretical significance. While industrial psychologists deal almost exclusively with observable behavior, neuroscientists study the brain's hard-wiring, the electrical impulses that fire when we are excited into thought or action. Neuroeconomics is devoted to studying these brain functions in order to understand why and how we make our decisions, particularly under stress. At Duke, Huettel and his associates ask their subjects to play card games involving risk decisions, or they ask them to make decisions while measuring their brain patterns with functional magnetic resonance imaging (fMRI). These fMRIs allow the different brain areas to be monitored as they respond to decisions and stresses.

Of course, people are infinitely complex, no behaviors are absolute, and neuroeconomics is in its infancy. And, some people do indeed overcome panic during a crisis and are able to keep the long-term interest of the company in mind. However, Huettel believes that these exceptions, if anything, prove the rule.

"The absolute key thing to keep in mind is that these sorts of biases are very resistant to willful change," Huettel says. "Simply thinking that, because we're aware of them, we're going to turn them off is probably misguided.

"A better solution is to set up decision situations or even corporate institutions that prevent these sorts of biases from taking shape and taking hold," advises Huettel. As a leadership goal, "you want to put people in situations where they will make better decisions" as well as manage situations where you can reduce – reduce, because you cannot ultimately eliminate – the effects of the instinctual fear mechanisms.

For example:

Offer facts rather than bromides. An internal crisis communications strategy based on general reassurances is doomed from the outset. No matter how many ways you find to say, "Don't worry," everyone will worry. We are wired to process threats in terms of our personal, immediate survival, Huettel points out. We are all therefore inclined to personalize any crisis, even a crisis involving a company-wide issue that doesn't directly involve our own department. In the absence of specifics, the staff will create a story to fill in the blanks, probably magnifying the dangers in the process. They will quickly replace initiatives to save the company with actions to save themselves.

Leadership action: "Offer information in such a way that it encourages employees to appraise the problem in terms that aren't so emotionally evocative," advises Huettel. "Instead of sugar-coating a dangerous problem, you might say, 'Right now our company is in turmoil. But here is what we're doing, and here is how we stand compared with our peers. The consequences may impact our stock price, but we expect to save jobs.'"

Recognize where patterns exist – and don't exist. The ability to respond to observable natural patterns – the behavior of animals, weather changes, food availability – has been indispensable to our survival, which is precisely why neuroeconomists believe that the identification of patterns is part of our hard wiring. Applied to more abstract situations, however, this hard wiring can make us see patterns where they don't exist.

In Huettel's laboratory, for example, test subjects stubbornly indentify patterns in cards dealt to them at random. In the outside world, imagined patterns in the ups and downs of stocks and bonds lead hopeful investors to "time" the markets no more intelligently than bettors assure themselves they can divine the next winner at Churchill Downs.

During a corporate crisis, pattern identification can be useful, say, in identifying the root cause of a technical problem, finding which departments or individuals may be contributing to the crisis, or anticipating the next moves of an adversary or competitor. But keep in mind that these observations create hypotheses, not conclusions. Responding before testing may only worsen the crisis at hand.

Leadership action: Encourage your advisers to identify all potentially relevant behavioral patterns they see within the organization as the critical situation develops. "But once people find the cause, you want to have ways of testing with hard data before relying on hunches," Huettel says. "You want to take advantage of the human mind's ability to find patterns, but also recognize that we have a lot of false positives."

During crises, for example, one might naturally expect the company's legal advisors to be overly cautious. It's a pattern supported by stereotype and assumption, but is it supported by facts? Does the legal department's past behavior actually suggest excessive caution or not? In this example, it is essential for leaders to know whether the presumed pattern actually exists if they are to properly evaluate whatever counsel the lawyers provide in the current crisis.

Fight the fixations. Surviving perilous situations requires identifying and acting on the most pressing threat. When you're struggling too far out in the surf, every thought and act is aimed at getting back to shore as quickly as possible. No matter how complex a crisis may be, our natural tendency is to simplify it; that is, to put it into terms that can define a direct and immediate response.

"In crisis, we fixate so much on one way of solving problems and looking at things that we miss other avenues and don't ever achieve the optimal solution," Huettel says.

As a result, some employees will focus on one problem to the exclusion of others, over-rely on established process, or avoid venturing creative decisions that entail risk. Even a swimmer too far off shore may have multiple solutions if, say, back-floating with the tide will work when strenuous exertion won't. In a business situation, the potential for alternative solutions is all the richer.

Committees don't generally increase the number of options at hand. Quite to the contrary, they tend to reinforce, rather than neutralize, organizational fixations. "Groups don't always make the best decisions," Huettel says. "Individuals who have similar biases can actually lead to worse overall decisions than individuals might [reach] on their own," since the power of numbers only tends to sanctify and concretize a bad decision, making it that much harder to overturn.

Leadership action: the tendency towards fixation, by individuals and groups, speaks directly to the need for checks and balances within an organization; in other words, concrete procedural systems for reviewing decisions and questioning long-held beliefs. "You've got to create a culture in which assumptions are questioned regularly," Huettel says.

Such a culture can only be created during peacetime, during those periods when the company is not facing a crisis. Once a crisis occurs, it's obviously way too late to set up a review system to qualify the very decisions that are already being made under duress.

Yet even beyond such practical reasons for acting early, when the seas are relatively mild, there are fundamentally qualitative reasons to do so, based on how the human brain itself responds to crises and works toward ways to best manage them. "When you look closely at the brain circuitry, there are certain areas that become more active when we are not immediately under stress. These areas involve creative, unconstrained thought," says Huettel.

"When we're facing a crisis, we don't tend to engage in that type of thinking. That can have negative consequences. In crisis, we sacrifice the big picture in order to focus on the here and now."

Peacetime is Big Picture Time. Don't waste it.

RULE NO. 17

HEROES ARE HARD TO FIND

If You Run into the Fire,
Be Prepared to Get Burned

In the fall of 2008, as once-mighty American International Group descended into turmoil amid the global financial crisis, Anastasia Kelly had every apparent reason to grab her impeccable reputation and head for the Exit sign.

Kelly had joined AIG as General Counsel just two years earlier to help the insurance giant recover from what then seemed like a defining crisis: a $1.6 billion settlement related to charges of accounting fraud and other irregularities. Throughout her storied career, Kelly had been sought for her steadying hand by troubled companies from Sears to MCI/WorldCom.

Yet few, if any, could have anticipated what lay in store for AIG in late 2008 and 2009 – that perfect storm of financial disaster and reputational mayhem, which led to AIG's becoming the world's most visible (and reviled) symbol of everything that went wrong before, during, and after the global meltdown. Not just shareholders, the entire country, and more than a few overseas nations as well, turned their wrath on AIG and its employees. While busloads of well-orchestrated protesters appeared at employees' homes and while outside consultants were literally attacked on the streets of New York because they forgot to remove their AIG identification tags, members of Congress were berating executives, including Kelly, in public hearings.

She had not caused the crisis, and she certainly didn't need the job. With Kelly's resume, she could have immediately landed another position at almost any company that had not been prejudged and condemned. Yet Kelly remained with AIG for another full year, leaving only in December 2009 after the darkest and most turbulent days were apparently over.

Like a true leader, she ran toward the fire, embracing more responsibility rather than less. In February 2009, she was promoted to Vice Chairman, overseeing not just the legal department but communications, human resources, and compliance. "I enjoy being at the forefront of the fray," she says, simply enough. "I always have."

As AIG found itself forced to respond on multiple fronts simultaneously, from Capitol Hill to Main Street, the abiding concern for Kelly was how to keep herself and a combined staff of the several thousand AIG workers under her direct authority motivated, focused, and productive in a time of unending disruption. It was certainly not easy to form an effective and cohesive response strategy at a large company with traditionally strong and clear divisions between different departments and areas.

According to Kelly, AIG was by no means exempt from the "silo culture" that we discuss elsewhere. (See Chapter 1, for example.) For example, if one department needed a quick response to some issue breaking on Capitol Hill, the resultant strategy first had to move through the government relations department, often at speeds too slow to meet the rapidly changing dynamics of the situation. As a result, says Kelly, "We were under criticism from a lot of different fronts, and we didn't have an organized approach."

Her new title overseeing multiple areas gave Kelly the authority, working with chief executives Edward Liddy and, subsequently, Robert Benmosche, to create cohesive interdepartmental crisis strategies. But the title alone wasn't going to be enough. Kelly knew she would have to draw on the experiences she'd had and the crisis strategies she developed at other companies to help guide AIG. Among the best practices that saw her through, Kelly now emphasizes:

Withholding information is not power. "I'm a big communicator. I want everybody at the table," Kelly says. "Some people feel that, if they have more information than somebody else, they have more power. I don't subscribe to that. If I have an issue, I want everyone from every constituency at the table hammering it out."

Every two weeks Kelly held an extensive meeting of her entire leadership team, which consisted of about 20 managers. "Everyone heard about everyone's issues and how they were being dealt with, so no one got blindsided. Lots of times at a company that size, you'll have people working on the same issue in different parts of the company. The last thing you want is for those people to be inconsistent with one another."

When the crisis broke, Kelly understood that just meeting with her own reports wouldn't ensure fluid communication among the AIG business units located around the world, many of whom were understandably in confusion about the crisis and the company's future. That's why Kelly launched "crisis meetings" to which she invited representatives from virtually every unit to attend, in person or by phone.

"We did these at first on a daily basis, then several times a week," she says. "We discussed the burning issues of the day with Legal, Communications, HR, Regulatory, and Government Affairs. We also invited different function or business leaders for different calls, depending on what was happening." Soon, these various leaders began speaking more openly with one another, even without formal meetings. The crisis meetings had fostered a new climate of cross-silo openness, helping AIG respond to the extraordinary pressures it faced.

Never a "my way or the highway" leader, Kelly prefers to hash things out until the group finds common ground. "I try to make decisions through consensus. But if, at the end, I don't have consensus, I don't mind making the call."

Organize and segment problems. A crisis, particularly one as protracted and multifaceted as AIG's, can easily overwhelm a staff. With so many problems to address, where does one begin? At the same time, extended crises can create a debilitating sense of non-achievement as each completed task is replaced by one or two fresh emergencies.

For Kelly, the only way to tackle big problems is to segment them and keep tracking each milestone you pass. "I've always been very organized and structured," she says. "When I was in college, each Sunday night I used to make lists of the things I wanted to accomplish during the week." Her roommates ribbed her for it, but such habits have helped her convert big crises into smaller, containable tasks.

"Every week, you should be pulling yourself up by the

bootstraps and saying, 'What was my week like? What did we accomplish? What was the goal? What did we get mired in? When you get so far into the weeds that you can't see where you're going, that's when you get bollixed up and you can't move."

Meet panic head-on. Kelly has been in enough crisis situations over the years to sense incipient panic in one of her employees almost immediately. "The only way to deal with it is direct intervention," she says. "I want people to come and tell me that. My door is always open. I'm always on email.

"We have so many issues that it's not like people are ringing false alarms. If there's a problem, I deal directly with the person involved and we work it out until we get to a place where they feel comfortable. If they still don't feel comfortable, we figure out who else we can bring in to address the issue."

Keep on an even keel. It's easier said than done, of course, when every day seems to bring a new twist. Kelly maintains her sense of balance (and, by extension, passes that sense along to her charges) by comparing a day at the office, however stressful, to life's greater concerns. "Nobody's dying," she'll observe, simply and eloquently enough.

"You can mentor people to put things in perspective, to understand that this is not the end of the world. This too shall pass. The best thing to do is to manage what's in front of you. That's all part of growing professionally and learning how not to get mired in the details."

"I try to deal with everything with a sense of humor," she says. Of course that doesn't mean taking important issues lightly or underestimating the scope of problem. But attitude and manageability are directly related. As Kelly says, "If you can't have a sense of humor about what's happening in your work life, I don't see how you can sustain it."

For crises such as the ones our world endured in 1932, or in 2009, a certain kind of leadership personality is as necessary as it is hard to find. The job description calls for people who will assume responsibility in a situation they know in advance will be thankless, who understand that they will be blamed for bad things that are not their fault even as they are ignored for good things that would have been impossible without them. Kelly was one of very few executives who fit that bill during the historic crisis of 2008-2009 – a leader when leadership was in perilously scarce supply.

SECTION FOUR

WASHINGTON, D.C.
The Epicenter of Power Today

Just over 30 years ago, Chrysler Corporation CEO Lee Iacocca appeared before the Congress in search of a bailout. While comparisons with more current events have not been scarce, it is still useful for our purposes here to recall the extraordinary back-and-forth between Iacocca and Sen. William Proxmire, then Chairman of the Senate Banking Committee, during public hearings on the matter.

"You are now asking the government to risk $12.5 billion," said Proxmire at one point. "If it fails, the taxpayer takes a painful bath. If it succeeds, you will be a famous success and be made very, very wealthy."

Proxmire also chided Iacocca for apparently contradicting his own laissez-faire philosophy by begging at the public trough. It was that era's version of the "capitalist on the way up, socialist on the way down" syndrome that we hear ascribed to 2008 bailout recipients. Iacocca ate that piece of crow and simply did not engage Proxmire along ideological lines. With respectful deference to Proxmire's agenda, he powerfully articulated the consequences for everyone if the government failed to act.

Senator Proxmire never did vote for the bailout but, at the end of the hearings, he told Iacocca, "... I have rarely heard a more eloquent, intelligent, well-informed witness... You did a brilliant job. We thank you."

Everyone's hands were therefore washed. It was a demonstration by Iacocca of corporate leadership as it is supposed to play out in Washington. His strategy has never been more relevant than it is today.

To be sure, Washington has always been an essential switch in the power circuit. No matter what the political climate, or which philosophies prevail in the White House and Congress, business leaders have long been lured to D.C. as an obvious place to seek favorable governmental actions, policies, and legislation. If not lured, they are often compelled to the journey whenever regulators and elected officials need to assess blame and rake a few private sector kingpins over the coals.

Today, however, the game is played on an elevated stage. On the one hand, voters distrust big government. On the other hand, they are apprehensive of unabashed plutocracy and they want it curbed. It's a tricky dynamic that elected officials must somehow navigate, commensurately trickier and more impactful in the wake of the economic crisis and the perception that government was asleep at the switch.

As such, it's a pretty fair bet that Washington will continue to be a more forceful player in business life regardless of election results. The days of the 1980s, when, for example, antitrust lawyers and enforcers were simply inactive, are gone for good.

Lee Iacocca gave us a hint of what kind of leadership this unprecedented pressure cooker requires, but its parameters also go beyond the demands that drove the events of 1979. In a general sense too, leadership can be harder to define in a context where the skill sets play out on a leveler playing field because they involve – not top-down commands – but negotiating, explaining, and lobbying.

Is that really leadership? You bet it is. The same communications skills that define leadership in the context of, say, internal corporate communications or spearheading major transactions with outside businesses, apply in refined form to how you talk to elected officials. Here too, leadership is all about reading the other guy's agenda, deciphering his or her (often hidden) needs, and finding a way to reach your own goals by helping others reach theirs.

Yet leadership in this context is often much more as well. Sometimes it's all about haunting the corridors of power in order to create whole groundswells, public and political, to achieve grand purposes. That's why, in this section, you will meet some of the best lobbyists in Washington. Like corporate CEOs, they know what buttons must be pushed and how to push them. Anyone who bases success on communications is a leader.

As we saw with Iacocca and Proxmire, businessmen and politicians often have uneasy relationships. Top-down managers can be frustrated by elected officials who need to balance multiple stakeholders and, at the end of the day, settle for less than ideal results. The first job of a politician is to survive, i.e., get reelected.

Meanwhile, in the current historical situation, the potential conflict is exacerbated a hundredfold. At a time when business is blamed for a massive economic and social crisis, how can politicians strike the right remedial balance? In turn, how can businesses work with politicians who must at least pose as their dire adversaries?

The good news is that so sharp an impasse presents historical opportunity. If, against such seemingly intractable odds, leaders from both the public and private sectors can achieve a more effective working dynamic, it will serve as a model of how their great respective powers can be harmoniously channeled during future crises. To paraphrase the popular song, if we can make it now, we can make it anytime!

The following pages offer just a few hints of that more effective public/private interaction, which is both possible and necessary in our post-TARP environment.

——————— RULE NO. 18 ———————
KNOWLEDGE IS POWER
Your Expertise Has Clout in Washington, So Use it Wisely

It's understandable that visitors to Washington, D.C. might perceive that power structure as a one-way street. After all, only legislators have the power to vote yea or nay on laws that dictate how the rest of us must act. At the same time, they seem to live in a world of their own, with personal agendas that are often hard to relate to the varied business interests of Main Street, America. That said, in order to be truly effective, legislators do always need one commodity that no constitutional authority can grant, but that you can provide in abundance: knowledge.

Former House Speaker Dennis Hastert puts it succinctly: "In government, knowledge is power."

A legislator's ability to bring specifics to a discussion or debate on a proposed bill is one of the key factors separating policy shapers – i.e., the leaders – from the followers in Washington. The knowledge that you as a corporate leader possess about your company, your industry, and compelling business and employment trends has tangible value to any legislators who hope to speak with authority and thereby enhance their own positions as people to be heeded, according to Hastert. In Hastert's case, his mastering the issues helped him attain and then hold the position of Speaker longer than any Republican in U.S. history.

"If you frame your argument to empower them, you can educate [legislators] about a certain aspect [of a bill] and give them the background to understand something better. That's power they can use [to help shape] the process," says Hastert, who left the House in 2007 and now serves as Senior Advisor to the Washington law firm Dickstein Schapiro. This honest exchange of information and ideas will advance the interests of your company even as you empower the lawmakers.

To build the necessary trust for such a relationship, leaders boil down the art and science of communications to its absolute essence: one person speaking openly and directly with another. Too often corporate leaders damage their chances from the outset by misreading the needs and motives of legislators, by asking for help without offering knowledge in return, or by simply forgetting to acknowledge and understand the human being behind the title.

"They might have a title, but they are people," Hastert says. "They have families, mortgages, responsibilities, and they try to do the best they can with the time they have." In more than 20 years in the House, Hastert saw the best and worst tactics and strategies when it came to how business leaders try to make themselves heard in Washington. Based on that experience, he offers the following suggestions:

Minimize pomp and circumstance. Hastert, a plain-spoken former high school wrestling and football coach, believes executives rely too heavily on elaborate gestures and formalities when engaging politicians.

"Sometimes a cup of coffee does as much good as a whole dinner," Hastert says. "A lot of people feel like they've got to come in and impress and over-persuade. They want to impress people with their knowledge of politics. Politicians can see through that like anyone else. Most people can spot a phony.

"If you really want to make an impression, you take a person at face value, sit down, and talk to them. You don't have to tell them what your degrees are in or how powerful you are. You're there because you want to effect a change. Explain why."

Make friends before making requests. "Just touching base can be important," Hastert says. "It doesn't hurt, when you're in Washington, to pick out a couple of people you want to see. Tell them why your business is important to their area, and don't ask for anything. Then, when you want something or need their help, at least you've built that relationship."

Get to know their staff. Given the number of constituents with whom politicians must deal, they are totally reliant on their staffs to steer them toward whatever must get their attention soonest. If you convince the chief of staff that your matter has important implications, you'll have the ear of the legislator.

Know the politician's story. "As most CEOs know, any success you can have depends on how you related to somebody," Hastert comments. It seems elemental to do a bit of background but, in his years in Congress, Hastert was always surprised at the number of CEOs who came to Washington intent on making themselves heard and achieving their corporate goals – without first bothering to learn the backgrounds of the people with whom they were dealing even though they were lobbying on issues critical to their businesses.

"First of all, you have to realize who's pulling the levers around here," says Hastert. "Today, you have to face the fact that your chairmen are going to be Democrats who probably came up through a Democratic organization position or came up through the union hierarchy, and that's how they got where they're at. On the other hand, if you're talking to a Republican, you're probably taking to a small business owner.

"You have to really understand two things: where this person's come from and why they're there," adds Hastert. "It gives you a frame of reference for how to deal with them and how to communicate. Secondly, look at the committees they're on and what they are trying to do. Try to frame your own objectives within the context of what their goals are."

While Republicans and Democrats may view issues from divergent perspectives, in the end most are seeking answers that benefit their constituents, Hastert says. Without being deceptive or disingenuous in the least, you can tailor your argument accordingly. "If you're talking to a Democrat, you might want to talk about creating jobs. If you're talking to somebody who's pretty conservative, you might want to talk about the free enterprise system. So it behooves you to know who you're talking to and what their background is, and frame it all around how you're going to create the better good."

----------------- RULE No. 19 -----------------

COOPERATE, COOPERATE, COOPERATE

When Dealing With Lawmakers, Focus on Details, Not Policy

Ask the CEO of a major company to describe what happens when Washington, D.C. politicians try to micromanage businesses through legislation. He or she may write you a book – or else just utter the two words "Sarbanes-Oxley."

Formally known as Section 404 and informally as Sarbox, the 2002 legislation, enacted on the heels of Enron and other corporate accounting scandals, is the contemporary bête noir of free market philosophers.

As the swift prosecutions of the late Enron CEO Ken Lay and other leaders engaged in malfeasance make clear, there were already laws on the books to deal with the out-and-out fraud that Enron and others perpetrated. From a free marketer's perspective, Sarbanes-Oxley has succeeded mainly in saddling thousands of honest, publicly traded companies with onerous, complex, even serpentine requirements for internal accounting. The largest companies now pay millions of dollars each year just to comply with Sarbox and a whole cottage industry of consultants has arisen, specialized in helping businesses try to understand and comply with the rules.

There's little doubt that well-meaning legislation places enormous burdens of companies. A 2009 article in *Policy Review* magazine noted that, in the years since President Reagan made regulation reduction a top priority for his administration, regulation has only grown under Democrat and Republican administrations alike. In fact, according to *Policy Review*, Washington's regulatory staffers grew by 38 percent between 2000 and 2004 to nearly 240,000 full-time equivalent employees.

Some companies do better than others in recognizing political realities and in managing the inevitable, unwanted circumstances to their own benefit. A 2006 study by Lord & Benoit (one of those consulting firms that help companies deal with the legislation) compared nearly 2,500 publicly traded companies according to two criteria: how well they had implemented accounting controls to deal with Sarbox and how their stock price has fared. The study found that the stocks of companies with effective controls during the first two years of the law rose nearly 28 percent, compared with the Russell Index average of 18 percent. By contrast, those that failed to implement such controls saw their stock price drop by 5.75

percent.

The lesson is clear. Love or hate the legislation, it is here and it is not going away any time soon. Get on board and deal with it and your company can prosper. Ignore or fight or delay dealing with the unavoidable huge headache and your company will likely suffer.

Legislators pass laws. By definition, that's what they do; that's how they respond to crises, perceived crises, and public outcries to "do something" about a problem. Often, they simply cannot afford to consider the longer-term consequences of their legislation, especially when their own survival requires a show of action.

"Many politicians don't even understand the legislation they're enacting and the ramifications of it," says Thomas C. Green, a partner in the Washington law firm of Sidley Austin LLP and a nationally recognized trial lawyer who frequently works with corporate executives in criminal and civil white collar cases. "The penalties attached to corporate crime have been ratcheted up and up over the last few years. I'm not here to engage in social commentary and address the wisdom of that," he adds. "Suffice it to say that, rather than finding ways to interface with the corporate community and ensure that regulation is efficient and working, we just kind of ratchet up penalties."

If Enron provided a catalyst for new laws, the financial meltdown in 2008 and early 2009 created a perfect storm of regulatory opportunity. "From the public's perception, there were a lot of corporations that misbehaved, and that translates into the political objective," he adds. "Obviously, there's a lot more regulation across the board.... The SEC's already reorganized in the aftermath of the Bernie Madoff debacle and Congress certainly has an appetite for new and additional regulation in the financial community." (Subsequent to Mr. Green's comments, legislation fundamentally overhauling regulation of the nation's financial markets was approved by the U.S. Senate in a 60-39 vote.)

As a CEO, you may want to marginalize the effects of Washington on your business. However, working with the Power nearly always trumps fighting against the Power. General Electric is a primary example. By serving on President Obama's Economic Recovery Advisory Board, Chief Executive Jeffrey Immelt put himself in a position not just to share his business expertise with the President but, presumably, to diplomatically highlight initiatives or new regulations that might unduly strap GE or business in general.

"Any prudent corporate executive needs to take account of the atmosphere that exists now, and which is likely to continue," Green says. "That means committing considerable effort to compliance and oversight."

One may rightly ask, if the legislators themselves don't understand the intricacies of the laws they themselves pass, how are large corporations supposed to avoid violations? Put simply, you can't. Not all the time, anyway.

"Corporations are huge organizations. No chief executive can police every employee and subordinate," Green says. "The truth is that, notwithstanding the best and most attentive commitment to doing things right, there will be people [in a company] who do things wrong."

Nowhere more than in Washington, D.C. does perception spell the difference between whether investigators give you the benefit of the doubt or use any violation as a pretext for a full-scale inquiry into your company and operations. "The way out of that dilemma, always, is to be able to demonstrate to any investigating authority that you were diligent, you were vigilant.

You did have all your compliance programs and activities in place, and this particular incident was one that simply could not have been detected or foreseen," advises Green. "If that's the case, the corporation typically gets a pass."

As the leader, it's your job to set the tone, Green says. "It takes a lot of leadership at the top of the corporation because much of the moral and ethical tone of a corporation is set by its leaders. Employees take their cues from management."

However, being realistic about compliance and Beltway oversight does not mean that you must simply sit back and wait for the legislative juggernauts to drive your own corporate destiny. You can have impact. Senators and representatives and their staffs are not experts on your industry-specific issues. They rely on experts to help them craft laws, and you can be one of those experts.

"There's still a fair amount of access to committees [that are] considering enhanced regulations or changes in the regulatory scheme. And there is still access to their staffs," Green says.

"What you communicate has to be sensible. It's a waste of time to spend resources saying, 'No, you shouldn't regulate and change things,' because that [strategy] gets you nowhere," Green says. Instead, "pay attention to the intricacies of what legislators are proposing and react to that with specificity."

It's your job to find that seemingly innocuous three-sentence clause that could actually derail your corporate growth plans – but not because the lawmakers want to derail your corporate growth plans. As definitive practitioners of the Law of Unintended Consequences, the bill's drafters may have no idea the wording could hurt you. They may be only too happy to make changes to specific passages on your behalf.

Before you can hope to wield such influence, however, you must be willing to accept legislation as a fact of life rather than an obstacle to be overcome. As Thomas Green says, coming to grips with that reality "is probably the most self-protective thing a company can do."

──────── Rule No. 20 ────────
Sometimes, True Leaders Are Unseen
How Underdogs and Improbable Causes Can Prevail in Washington, D.C.

This is a tale about two powerful Washington, D.C. lobbyists, Paul Quinn and Jack Quinn. More than the same name, they share a common vision of the powerful contributions that lobbyists make – must make – to our society. They share the same unhappiness over current perceptions of their profession. And, they share strikingly similar views of many of the institutions, issues, and objectives with which they've been engaged during the past three decades.

Most of all, they share an implicit belief that lobbyists at their best are leaders, no less so than the business executives they represent and the elected officials they persuade.

Let's start with a couple of images that, to anyone who read newspapers in the 1970s, would once have seemed so unlikely as to be preposterous.

In March 2007, Ian Paisley, head of Northern Ireland's Democratic Unionist Party and, for decades, a rabidly anti-Catholic obstructionist, sat down with leaders of the Sinn Féin, including its charismatic Catholic leader Gerry Adams, to finalize an agreement for a new government. That government would eventually include Paisley as First Minister and Sinn Féin's Martin McGuiness as deputy First Minister. A month later, Paisley was shaking hands with Dublin's Bertie Ahern, which he had vowed never to do until there was peace in Northern Ireland.

Ask most informed Americans to credit a U.S. politician for this monumental transformation, and they will quite appropriately name George Mitchell, the former Senate Majority Leader who, as United States Special Envoy for Northern Ireland, chaired the negotiations that led to the Belfast Peace Agreement. For that signal document – signed on Good Friday 1998 and now known as the "Good Friday Agreement" – everyone credits Mitchell's leadership. Everyone knows his personal intervention was critical.

What most Americans don't know is that, sixteen years earlier, it was a lobbying initiative spearheaded by Paul Quinn – dubbed the "Dean of Irish-American lobbyists" – that first paved the way toward peace in Northern Ireland, at a time when there was little interest in Washington in the woes of that small country. If anything, there was widespread conviction that the problems there were insoluble and that any effort to intervene would disserve U.S. interests.

Quinn's involvement with Ireland began innocuously enough in the early 1960s when his representation of the U.S. travel and tourism industry led to his working closely with the Irish government. A decade later, conditions in Belfast and Derry were mired in a tripartite standoff between local Protestants, local Catholics, and the British government. The Bloody Sunday massacre of 1972, which claimed the lives of 27 unarmed protesters including seven teenagers, was just one searing moment of The Troubles.

By 1982, Quinn had set about the task of assembling a nucleus of third-party supporters who could be deployed in both grassroots and behind-the-scenes efforts to convince the U.S. government that a presumably insoluble civil war was, in fact, a soluble political situation. First, though, he'd have to convince his own supporters, who were sympathetic enough but not necessarily so confident that Beltway opinion was malleable or conditions in Northern Ireland correctable.

Quinn's first key move was to formally embody the lobbying effort; in other words, to create a functional resource and agency to enhance understanding of what was happening in Northern Ireland, to maximize dialogue among key influencers, and to feel a way toward collective solutions. The organization was the Committee for a New Ireland and, under its aegis, members of Congress and Congressional staffers visited Ireland and Northern Ireland several times to meet with political and community leaders in both nations.

"Stateside, our biggest practical problem was the State Department," says Quinn. "It was at the time a decidedly Anglophile institution with no real sympathy for the people over there. And they had all kinds of purported policy reasons to support their predispositions. The unmistakable message was, 'We have no business in North Ireland.'

"Since very few people were addressing Irish issues in the United States at the time, the State Department was under no pressure to reconsider."

Quinn's winning strategy was to isolate the State Department by going directly to Congress – something a practiced lobbyist was best suited to do. In that endeavor, Quinn identified key supporters like Tom Hughes, Chief of Staff for Rhode Island Sen. Claiborne Pell. (Quinn is a Rhode Island native who had also served on Pell's staff earlier in his career.) Support from Sen. Edward Kennedy and House Speaker Tip O'Neill was likewise decisive as, for example, both men arranged for Quinn's introduction to John Hume, founding member of the Social Democratic and Labour Party and, with Ulster Unionist

Party leader David Trimble, co-recipient of the 1998 Nobel Peace Prize.

The Committee for a New Ireland would soon grow powerful enough to ignite a historical series of events. It garnered sufficient support on the Hill to pressure the British to enter into the 1985 Anglo-Irish Agreement – over the objections of the British Foreign Office and the reluctance of the U.S. State Department.

If nothing else, that treaty created the International Fund for Ireland, which would prove decisive. At first a mechanism for economic aid, the fund would also be a platform for international participation in the peace process and a fillip to Clinton administration efforts to negotiate a resolution. As Quinn worked closely with the President and First Lady to arrange their 1995 trip to Belfast and Derry, the stage was thus set for the appointment of Special Envoy George Mitchell and the culminating Good Friday Agreement of 1998.

This tale of how Paul Quinn and a handful of colleagues redefined a political landscape in Washington, D.C. underscores a number of lessons about leadership in general and lobbyists in particular. In a world motoring on instant gratification, the faithful patience required for success, when success really matters, is formidable. Quinn began his campaign in 1982, and the Good Friday Agreement was not signed until 1998. Another nine years would then elapse until Paisley's fateful handshake with Ahern.

Not just patience, the leadership here was also about resolute commitment to underdogs in a cause that presented very little reason for hope. Such commitment is particularly striking in light of the dim view most Americans take of lobbyists, post-Jack Abramoff, and ongoing public perceptions of "government relations" professionals as secretive, greedy, and ethically challenged at every juncture.

Post-Abramoff, we might do well to simply speculate on the number of human lives that have been saved because lobbyists doggedly pursued a specific objective for decades.

"Lobbyists fill voids," says Quinn, now a government relations partner at Nossaman LLP. "Without lobbyists acting as intermediaries – and I'm including the lobbyists who represent the world's Goliaths as well as its Davids – the process would simply be much less efficient."

"Complex issues would not otherwise be understood or become part of the public dialogue," adds Quinn. Translated into a business context, we're talking, for example, about technology issues that directly affect entrepreneurs and either encourage or discourage innovation. That's been another significant professional arena for Quinn, who labored hard to help deregulate AT&T and open diverse other frontiers for new players across the technology spectrum.

"Imagine a guy who grabs his cell phone to tell his daughter to be sure and watch a show on cable TV that he thinks will interest her," says Quinn. "Maybe the show is a talking heads panel discussion about the corruption wreaked on our system by lobbyists. But, without lobbyists, there might not have been either cell phones or cable. There would still be one lumbering telecommunications giant and three major networks, and very little competition or innovation."

"What we do is a form of advocacy," says Quinn. "We explain. We tell stories. We communicate. The monopolists have their lobbyists too, so the public can decide between what they're doing and what we're doing, just like they vote for candidates in an election."

Has the value of what lobbyists do ever been effectively communicated to the average citizen? "I haven't seen that it has, unfortunately," says Quinn, "and there lies the next great leadership challenge for my profession.

"For starters, we must impress on President Obama that his periodic attacks on lobbyists are counter-productive, unfair, and all the more frustrating when we consider that he too is a great advocate on the side of the underdog. But unfounded and extreme attacks on lobbyists breed cynicism and make it all the more difficult for us to fight worthwhile but sometimes unpopular causes."

"We must then establish some kind of forum – bipartisan, of course – to communicate the value of our work." Quinn adds, "In a sense, as advocates, we're ahead of the politicians themselves. My experience, with Ireland, with the AT&T break-up, and many other similarly important issues, is that we are often the first to sense implicit public demand. The fact that the public itself might not have yet formed its own conscious opinion makes our work all the more important.

"After all, we don't have to get reelected. We don't have to back down…and there are always new and different challenges to meet."

Imagine a polling of Americans in the days or months or years following the December 1988 terrorist bombing of Pan Flight 103 over Lockerbie, Scotland. The question: should the families of the people who died in that atrocity be generously compensated by Libya for their losses? No doubt such a poll would have shown an overwhelming mandate in favor. A U.S. Congressman would have been politically suicidal to oppose such a proposal. After all, it was fairly determined that Libya caused the tragedy.

Yet it wasn't until nearly 20 years to the day after the attack that those families finally received full compensation from the Libyan government. Much of that delay was due, of course, to the post-bombing hostilities with Libya, as well as the need to unequivocally establish Libya's culpability. Yet it's a powerfully important fact of recent American history that a web of U.S. government policy objectives and machinations also stood in the way of a just resolution.

The leadership role that lobbyists play in Washington is, in part, a patient effort to cut through such tangles in our own government in order to achieve clear objectives. Jack Quinn, of Quinn Gillespie & Associates LLC (QGA), spent three years doing precisely that on behalf of the Lockerbie families.

In this context, the leadership dance for lobbyists includes two different, equally crucial steps. First, they must understand what the blockage is, why it exists, and if it is indeed surmountable. Second, they need to work around the blockage as much as possible even while seizing every opportunity to push until it breaks. At all times, they need to determine when it's best to conciliate real or potential opposition, or whether a cudgel is called for.

For Jack Quinn, the problem on the U.S. end of the process was the State Department – even as it had been for Paul Quinn. Here, though, it was not a matter of cultural animosity or political indifference. Starting in the 1990s and continuing into the 21st century, "there was a legitimate need to seek rapprochement with Libya," says Jack Quinn. Especially as hostile powers consolidated their hold in Iran, and that nation began to rattle its incipient nuclear saber, "the clear policy decision was to work with Libya to further isolate Iran and create a bargaining wedge for the West."

Given this dynamic, Quinn's task was to constantly remind policymakers and lawmakers that the Lockerbie families were not opposed to this foreign policy strategy "but that that strategy should also not interfere with the legitimate claims of the families. The strategy, in other words, should not be implemented at their expense."

The delicate task was thus to bifurcate two significant components of the same volatile situation while simultaneously leveraging both to achieve Quinn's purpose. Again, Quinn argued, while the families were not opposed to rapprochement, their just demands, if ignored, could only obtrude on U.S. policy goals. A signal event was the successful pressure that Quinn exerted on members of the House Appropriations Committee to block the building of a new embassy in Tripoli.

Continuing pressure was felt by both the State Department and Libya. Quinn created what he calls an "echo chamber," such that "State could simply not talk to Congress without the subject of the Lockerbie families coming up."

Upshot: the State Department told Libya that the issue absolutely had to be resolved and Libya eventually set up a fund that was also embodied in a Congressional statute.

"The lobbyist's right to petition the government goes back to this country's founding," reflects Quinn, a veteran advisor to Democratic leaders and Counsel to the President of the United States from 1995 to 1997. Before the Clinton appointment, Quinn had been Vice President Al Gore's Chief of Staff and Counselor since 1993. "It is free speech actuated" – in other words, free speech that actually achieves a specific end beyond self-expression.

"From a practical standpoint, it is also a search for the truth that requires maximum input from stakeholders with opposing opinions and opposing interests," adds Quinn. "Congress' job is to sort out what my clients say and want from what our opponents say and want. It's all about creating a balance."

Again, the process must entail proportionate representation for the Goliaths perennially lumbering around Capitol Hill, although, like Paul Quinn, Jack Quinn seems to instinctively understand the leadership role of lobbyists more in terms of underdogs. He too includes among those underdogs all the innovators whose transformational new inventions and enterprises would have fallen by the wayside but for lobbyists who fought to loosen the chokeholds of the old technology behemoths.

At the same time, underdogs represent an extremely diverse populace on the Hill. Among such representations, Quinn mentions the relief he's been seeking for the Broadway theater industry – similar to the supports provided film industry interests – and not just for them, but also for all the small community playhouses that depend on road shows for their survival.

Even as brand-name Beltway players like Quinn Gillespie provide a voice for those who might not otherwise have one, recent history adumbrates their efforts. "I don't know if in my lifetime we will ever get rid of Jack Abramoff's shadow," says Quinn. Trial lawyers can get away with representing the malefactors of great wealth – it's their solemn duty under legal canon – but lobbyists are not respected for, or even excused for, such zealous advocacy on behalf of presumably inimical corporate interests. Like Paul Quinn, Jack Quinn is also disappointed by President Obama's contributions to the public vilification of powerful lobbyists.

"The situation will only get worse if law firms and public relations firms do our job instead of us," says Jack Quinn. "It will undermine the legitimate reins imposed by the Lobbying Disclosure Act because lobbying work will be done by people who don't need to register as lobbyists. The process will become uncontrolled. It will be legal, but bad for our society."

Quinn urges that lobbyists themselves get in front of the

reform issue. As we see so many times at every level of our nation's economic and political life, companies and entire professions become leaders by providing solutions to the very problems they're perceived to have caused. For lobbyists, Quinn especially advises his colleagues to take an aggressive – and conspicuous – part in barring contributions to Congressional committee members by anyone seeking anything from their committees. The prohibition would extend to both lobbyists and their clients.

"It's something we must do for ourselves *even if the effort fails*," says Quinn (emphasis added). "We need to make every real effort to succeed but, if we don't succeed, at least we have sent a message about ourselves that desperately needs to be sent. And, of course, such a campaign must absolutely be bi-partisan."

Generally speaking, though, bi-partisanship can send a potentially ambiguous message if it feeds cynical perceptions that lobbyists, far from standing for principle, are happy to sell their services to the highest bidders, be they Democrats, Republicans, or Mugwumps. In fact, Quinn Gillespie itself might be perceived as a prime example. QGA's co-founder is Ed Gillespie, who's been as prominent on the Republican side in the last few decades as Quinn has been on the Democratic.

"It's a very legitimate concern for which firms like our own have a very legitimate response," says Quinn. "The Democrats on our staff work as passionately for their causes and principles as any activist on the Hill, as do our Republicans," says Quinn. "But there are enormous benefits for all our clients when both sides work under one roof because the professionals on the opposing end of the political spectrum can always provide a crucial reality check."

If, for example, the Democrats are zealously pursuing an ultra-liberal objective, the Republicans are there to say, "Wait a minute, that won't fly. You'll never succeed. Here's how you moderate your campaign to get the most that you possibly can for the client." When the Republicans at QGA likewise push the envelope on behalf of their clients, the Democrats return the favor.

"Again," says Quinn, "it's all about balance."

For all the scathing attacks on the profession, there's good news for the future of government relations. "So many young people are still coming to Washington to join our ranks," says Paul Quinn. "There's never been a greater interest and enthusiasm. Never have so many of the best and brightest knocked on our doors."

Yet the most serious leadership problem now haunting Washington, D.C. falls well beyond the power of any lobbyist to solve. Talk to Beltway veterans, to the politicos and lobbyists and lawyers who've served here for decades; the same miasma haunts them all. Will the atmosphere in Washington ever improve? Can respect and bipartisanship be restored? Can't we all just get along, to coin a phrase?

Paul Quinn and Jack Quinn use remarkably similar tone and language in their assessment of the prospects for such renewal. "I wish I could be more optimistic," says Paul Quinn. "But the age of Talk Radio isn't going away, and I'm not sure that any leadership effort to establish common ground won't be rebuffed."

"Sadly, I cannot be optimistic," says Jack Quinn. "Forty years of redistricting have hardened the problem, so that Congressional districts are all pretty much ideological fortresses. You've got these heavily Democratic districts where there's no political advantage for the representative to care about the Chamber of Commerce. And you've got these reshaped Republican districts where there's no political advantage for the representative to care about the NAACP."

The leadership needed to overcome the electorate's headlong plunge into tribal silos may or may not be possible. There are, however, political leaders in our recent past who do at least provide a model of the bipartisan instinct that's now such a public service imperative. In the next chapter, we'll talk to one of them.

—————————— RULE NO. 21 ——————————

CONSENSUS-BUILDING DEMANDS UNPRECEDENTED LEADERSHIP

In an Embittered World, the Search for Bipartisan Comity Continues

Talk to people in Washington, D.C. – especially the Beltway veterans who remember a political culture in which it was common practice to reach across the aisle in pursuit of the greatest good for the greatest number – and they're usually too honest to pretend they entertain great hopes that the rancor of recent years will somehow soften into respectful collegiality any time soon.

Yet today's leadership challenge consists in precisely this endeavor to forge consensus in a world where a combination of permanent election cycles, media demagoguery, and painful "social issues" make such consensus all the more difficult to even imagine. Some politicos wistfully remember the likes of Sen. Henry ("Scoop") Jackson, who made their living by creating common ground. The question is: are there consensus-makers still among us? What does leadership in this context look like in today's world?

Throughout his political career as a U.S. Representative and

Senator from Maine, and as a Republican Secretary of Defense in the Democratic Clinton Administration, William S. Cohen developed an exemplary reputation as a leader able to put partisan differences aside in the interest of greater collective benefits.

At the same time, Cohen never confused compromise with capitulation on matters of principle, regardless of the parties or interests involved. In the early 1970s, during his first term in the House, Cohen made one of the difficult decisions of his life, breaking with members of his own party to support the impeachment of President Nixon.

"My entry into politics was on a nonpartisan basis," Cohen says. "I ran for City Council in Bangor, Maine. You didn't run with a party label. If you had a pro- or anti-business attitude, they would know whether you were left wing or right wing, but there was no partisanship in terms of organizing your campaign. You were simply 'Cohen for City Council' or 'Cohen for Mayor.' I learned something during that experience in terms of building a consensus to achieve the best results."

By the time he decided to run for Congress in 1972, Cohen was a declared Republican. Yet instead of targeting population centers most likely to support his views, Cohen undertook the monumental task of walking the entire 2nd district – nearly 28,000 square miles and geographically the largest congressional district east of the Mississippi River.

He stayed each night with a different family. "They would host a dinner for three, four, five, or 10 people, and then there would be a discussion until midnight. And I was back on the road the next day at 6 a.m., walking until 8 p.m.

"I particularly made an effort to go into areas known to be hostile or not receptive to Republicans," he adds. Working class Lewiston, then home to shoe factories and textile mills, was known as a Democrat stronghold of predominantly Franco-American voters. Many of the older residents spoke mainly French, so Cohen printed his campaign literature for the city in both French and English. "I wanted to make sure they read my message in the language they were most comfortable in," he says.

"All of my Republican colleagues said don't waste your time, because they're never going to vote Republican," Cohen adds. Yet by overcoming his own party's stereotypes about Democrats, he could overcome the voters' stereotypes about him.

"The people of Lewiston turned out to have strong conservative principles. They were getting caught up in the label that Republicans only care about business, while Democrats only care about people. I said that's not true, Republicans care just as much about people, they just have a different way of generating opportunities," he says. Although he didn't carry Lewiston in his first successful bid for Congress, "I narrowed the deficit in terms of what Republicans had achieved there before, and eventually I started winning Lewiston."

As a leader looking for the best staff and advisor he could find, Cohen says he demanded no party loyalty or ideological bent. "I had no idea what their political affiliation was. I hired the best people I could find, people who would be loyal to me in terms of my mission, my goals for what I wanted to achieve legislatively. I was less concerned about what their political opinions might be. I wanted to know how smart they were and whether they were willing to work with me. I can handle the diversity of their opinions and be better for it."

It's that trait he most admires in one of his greatest leadership models, Abraham Lincoln. "He was confident enough in his own abilities that he could bring people into his cabinet who formerly had challenged him. That is the mark of a great leader."

After leaving the Pentagon in 2001, Cohen launched a

corporate advisory firm, The Cohen Group, to help large companies extend their businesses internationally. As Cohen has found, the same principles that helped him gain common ground with adversaries in politics apply directly to the process of companies expanding overseas.

Companies that have the most difficulty achieving success in foreign markets are those that enter the markets out of a desire to expand, or to stay on par with competitors – but without taking the time and care to understand that country, its cultures, and values.

"You've got to be willing to understand the culture of the country," he says. "What are its needs? They will want to know who you are, why you are here, and what it is that you have to offer them." Corporate leaders have to be very sensitive to culture and history, so that you're in a position to identify and talk to the right ministers. Who are they, what is their background, what is the economic climate, and what do they hope to achieve by allowing entry into their markets?

Of course, the CEO will delegate many of the required tasks to a competent team. But there's no substituting for deep, personal involvement from the top. "You've got to ask, is this an appropriate mission, what are the barriers, and what price do we have to pay? If we're a public company, how do we rationalize this in such a way that's acceptable to shareholders?

"But the [really] tyrannous aspect for a CEO is time," Cohen said. "At a major company, time is real money, and there are so many demands on the leader." The idea of flying off to India for face time may be difficult to contemplate. All the more reason, Cohen points out, for your company to be absolutely certain that this venture is in its long-term interests and essential to its long-term strategy.

"They will want to see you," Cohen says. "They need to

have your face associated in their mind's eye with this company, and to know that you are committed to this project, and that they can trust you. That is the key to all of this. Your reputation for honesty, honor, and quality. If any of those are called into question, it's almost impossible to recover."

Here too, Cohen is reminded of how important simple legwork was during his 1972 campaign and his decision to sit down with the people of Lewiston and print his literature in a language they could best understand.

SECTION FIVE

BOARDS
New Liability, New Leadership

B ack in 1996, a *New York Times* business article was still able to cite a phenomenon called "trophy directors," referring to celebrated individuals from the corporate or political arenas who serve on the boards of a dozen or more corporations. Such a directorship was almost the equivalent of a private mobile brand, as the persons so dubbed had the name recognition, cachet, connections, and presumed sagacity to qualify them as prized additions to any boardroom. They simply needed to take a seat at the table.

Today, few, if any, individuals carry sufficient weight to succeed in the boardroom on reputation alone. It's no reflection on them; it's rather that the expectations have changed. Today, the responsibilities are daunting. Individual board members can no longer rely on their own independent brands but must instead fully align themselves with the brands of the companies they serve. In other words, they must provide deeper service on fewer boards. They must take the time to learn, study, ask questions, and provide hands-on governance to a degree previously unheard of.

Shareholder activists, regulators, and policymakers are demanding that directors take an abiding interest in the companies they serve – or face removal or even, in some cases, personal liability if the company fails. With new governance guidelines in place or on the way, board members may well find themselves competing with other directorship candidates and facing battles for reelection. It's a far cry from the days when boards showed up for a few annual meetings, ate dinner, and essentially rubber-stamped the important management decisions presented for their approval.

Even as the old system fostered boardroom collegiality, it concentrated power in the hands of the chief executive. There was little incentive for directors to act independently, to ask probing questions, or to fulfill their role as guardians of shareholder interests.

"Twenty years ago, being on a board wasn't viewed as much of a job, to be honest," says Richard H. Koppes, Of Counsel for the global corporate law firm Jones Day and a specialist in governance. Koppes has advised a veritable Who's Who of Fortune 500 companies on governance matters, taught governance at Stanford University, and served as a director for a number of major corporations and organizations himself. "Boards have become much more empowered in the last decade," he says. "Their relationship with the C-suite has intensified."

Board members unaware that the new century had ushered in a culture of board responsibility suffered a rude wake-up call in 2002 with the case of telecommunications giant WorldCom and its charismatic CEO Bernie Ebbers. Among those who fell hardest for the patented Ebbers charm were the company's directors, one of whom reportedly referred to him in private as "God" and "Superman". Nobody seemed more surprised than the board when Ebbers and his top lieutenants turned out to have perpetrated a massive accounting fraud that ultimately cost the company and its shareholders billions of dollars and resulted in what was then the largest bankruptcy in American history.

Though directors were not directly implicated in the crimes that earned Ebbers a 25-year jail sentence, investigations made public a slew of embarrassing board lapses. In the end, courts found 10 former directors *personally liable* for a portion of WorldCom's demise, ordering them to pay a total of $18 million out of their own pockets, or about 20 percent of their combined personal net worth. The ruling signaled more than just outrage over one company's wrongdoings. It brought to a swift and decisive end the age of corporate directorship as merely an honorary title.

The new, more active, and weightier role played by board members is directly tied to the ascendance of shareholder power in corporate decision making. Think of the power structure in a publicly traded company as a triangle. On one point, you have management; on the second, the board; and, on the third, the shareholders who own the company. "That's the governance paradigm in this country," Koppes says. Today, institutional shareholders representing large chunks of stock are demanding far greater accountability in the way companies are managed. They want a greater voice in selecting directors and they're not shy about holding their feet to the fire on such matters as executive pay, ensuring strict compliance with accounting and other laws, and seeing to it that corporate moves such as acquisitions and expansions are designed to serve sound corporate strategy rather than the chief executive's ego. That, in turn, magnifies the expectations incumbent on anyone who agrees to serve on a board.

Says Koppes, "Being a director today is a job. It's work. It's serious work. It's much more intense."

—————————— RULE NO. 22 ——————————

YOU MUST DIRECT AND TRANSFORM THE COMPANY, AT LEAST FOR NOW

When Major Challenges Arise,
Oversight May Not Be Enough

We've seen the perils of board passivity, and we've insisted on the need for board members to ask tough questions and hold senior managers to account. Sometimes, though, even that's not enough. When scandal engulfs tops managers, board members must, in essence, prepare to direct and transform the company for as long as it takes to resolve bet-the-farm issues and stabilize the organization.

Edward A. Kangas, who serves on the boards of several prominent companies, faced just such a situation when he was asked in 2003 to serve as chairman of Tenet Healthcare Corp. amid a Medicare payment scandal threatening the company. Tenet, one of the largest private hospital companies in the United States, had been taking advantage of a loophole in the Medicare payment system, to maximize "outlier payments," which are what Medicare pays to treat the most seriously ill patients.

The company ultimately paid $900 million to the U.S. government to settle the matter. More serious, potentially, was the damage to the company's reputation and its ability to continue functioning, as most of its top managers, including the CEO, had to be replaced. Kangas was recruited to the board and asked to be non-executive chairman to lead the board through the crisis.

Among his first steps as chairman was to visit some of Tenet's hospitals, to speak individually with front-line doctors, nurses, and administrators. He was struck mainly by their professionalism and their deep commitment to the patients under their care. "I had to assess whether this company was corrupt. It was not, it was made up of very good people," Kangas recalls. "This was a wonderful company with a lot of excellent people. The task at hand was a worthy endeavor.

"Management wasn't corrupt, either, but they had been affected by what I'll call 'Wall Street Medicine.' For-profit hospital companies do have a responsibility to shareholders for maximum performance, but the constituencies are a little broader. There are other stakeholders. It has to do with the quality of medicine and the care that's provided, regulatory compliance, and doing what's right."

Convinced of the underlying strength and soundness of the company, Kangas quickly set about helping the board install a new management team, starting with the CEO. After a broad search, the board settled upon Trevor Fetter, a former Tenet executive who had recently returned to the company to help during the crisis.

Ultimately, the board also replaced nine of its 11 directors. Burned by the scandal, many members had become cynical about the company. "They hadn't done such a bad job. But if the company was going to have the opportunity for a new day, it had to have a clean sweep," Kangas says.

Kangas is careful to note that directing and transforming a company should never be the board's long-term goal or responsibility. As quickly as possible, the CEO must be appointed and his or her managers must re-assume that role. "When things are difficult or fast-moving, employees need to be swift and laser-like, and they need a CEO who's empowered, whom people respond to," Kangas says. To underscore that point, Kangas is careful to refer to himself as a "non-executive chairman."

"I am not chairman of Tenet Healthcare, I'm chairman of the board of directors," he adds. "It's important for people to know who the leader is. Trevor Fetter is the leader of Tenet Healthcare inside and out. He is a great CEO, and he saved the company."

Yet there's no denying the crucial role that board members play during that brief-as-possible period when they must shoulder outsized responsibilities. "It doesn't take being tough, or being all that brilliant," Kangas says. "But it does take a certain courage. Courage sometimes means simply doing what's right even if it's difficult…. You'll have some opposition, or receive disparaging comments. You just have to have the courage to do what's right."

In 2004, Computer Associates (now called CA), one of the nation's leading IT companies, faced a similar situation. The company was engulfed in scandals involving accounting procedures, questionable compensation practices, and obstruction of justice. The company's directors, some newly appointed in the wake of the scandals, were thrust into a new role as they found themselves making critical decisions on personnel and operations.

One of the board's first moves was to hire Kenneth V. Handal as Executive Vice President, a highly experienced corporate risk and compliance attorney, to advise as they navigated the crisis. "I came into Computer Associates after almost the entire senior echelon had gotten fired," says Handal, who previously had served as compliance counsel for Altria, which was then the parent company of Kraft Foods and Philip Morris. "There were virtually no other senior officers.... I was hired by the then-chairman of the board, Lew Ranieri. Lew, his successor Bill McCracken, and the entire board were very active from that point forward in guiding the company through the troubles... and basically transformed the company."

Fortunately, the core business remained sound as enough customers were still satisfied with the company's products and services. Not surprisingly, given the scandal, the main need was to resurrect its reputation for ethical compliance. "There was a lot to do in terms of culture and integrity within the company," says Handal.

Not only were senior managers prosecuted as individuals (several went to jail), but the company itself faced possible charges stemming from the actions of management. Working closely with the board, Handal negotiated an agreement with prosecutors not to pursue charges against the company as long as it implemented sweeping reforms of its practices.

One early step the board took was to find and hire as CEO a leader of impeccable reputation, IBM veteran John A. Swainson, who would implement and reinforce ethical standards throughout the company. Among many changes to the board's own practices, directors decided to look much more closely than in the past at risk management, through a newly established compliance and risk committee.

Risk doesn't just refer to potential scandals. "You might have financial risks involving customers, or concerns about whether you're staying ahead of the game in terms of innovation," says Handal. "As with any company, you might have compliance risks. Or there could be political risks in going into certain countries overseas, or risk posed by competition or industry consolidation. Risk is everywhere."

Betsy Atkins, an entrepreneur and CEO of a venture capital investment company called Baja Corp., offers an even more dramatic example of how boards must sometimes assume 24/7 responsibility for corporate operations. Atkins has served on a number of boards over the years but, listening to her, we can safely surmise that her tenure as a director of HealthSouth – during a protracted crisis that made front-page headlines nationwide – stands out as a definitive experience even though she was only on the board for a little over two weeks in 2003.

Atkins knew when she joined that HealthSouth, a major healthcare company based in Birmingham, Ala., faced problems. In fact, she was appointed specifically as an independent director charged with investigating allegations of insider trading. The stakes increased exponentially when, just as Atkins took her seat, charges of criminal fraud against the company surfaced.

"Criminal fraud is a whole different matter from an allegation of insider trading," Atkins says. She led the board on daily calls. "It was more than a full-time job. It was a 16-hour-a-day job," Atkins recalls. "Every single day, we made a major decision, and we kept the company from going out of business. The company was in-the-zone-of-insolvency, as trading had been suspended on the New York Stock Exchange for four days. This was a company with 55,000 employees, a million patients, and about 3,000 hospitals. So it was really important that the customers – the patients – be cared for."

Atkins ultimately left the board after just 16 days when Chubb insurance terminated HealthSouth's D&O (directors and officers) insurance. By then, she says, the worst of it was over. "The overall outcome was positive because the company was able to keep functioning, service was provided to patients, and the company avoided bankruptcy," she adds.

While most boards will never have to face such problems, it's safe to say that the directors who accepted their positions at Tenet Healthcare, Computer Associates, and HealthSouth also never expected or had any intention to take day-to-day control of the company. As their experience shows, accepting the role of director means offering more than just vigilant oversight and wise counsel. It means that, on any given day, you might even have to take charge, and direct and transform the company.

RULE No. 23
How Directors Reward the CEO Says Everything
The Board's Defining Issue

You don't need a complex formula and endless data points to know if a board of directors is doing its job or acting irresponsibly. Just look at how (and how much) they're paying the chief executive, says Nell Minow, co-founder and chair of the Corporate Library and one of the leading shareholder advocates in the United States.

Minow says compensation goes right to the heart of how effective boards really are in protecting shareholder interests and holding management to rigorous standards. If they can stand up to the test on this issue, they can do so on virtually all other issues as well. "It's the most effective way to gauge how a board communicates with the executives about what its priorities are," says Minow.

The days are gone when CEOs, as board chairmen, could basically structure their own pay packages by comparing themselves to other highly paid CEO peer groups in the same industry. While peer comparison does still play a role, shareholder activists (not to mention the public, the media, and, increasingly, politicians) are demanding more modest salaries and incentives than in the past, and they want those salaries and incentives tied closely to the performance of the company. This trend has transformed the board's compensation committee from a cozy oasis into a potential minefield.

Following the collapse in 2008 of Bear Stearns and Lehman Brothers, which helped set in motion the global financial crisis, Minow testified before the House Committee on Oversight and Government Reform. She pointed out that, for several years prior to the collapse, her organization had given those firms' boards poor ratings, in part because of their habit of rewarding top executives for questionable performance.

Holding the line on corporate pay requires more than just being attentive and knowledgeable enough to know the difference between reasonable compensation and florid excess. It requires the plain toughness to directly confront a chief executive and deny raises or bonuses or even cut compensation when he or she has failed to meet goals. Standards will vary by industry and market conditions, but they should be clearly established and inviolable.

"If you say bonuses will be based on nine metrics, but it will be within the discretion of the board to award all of the bonus for achieving *any* of the metrics, you've basically said, 'we're imbeciles and we don't care,'" Minow observes. Sometimes, board members must have the temerity to limit pay even when the executive has worked diligently and performed well. If the company as a whole is suffering, employees who are enduring layoffs and stockholders who are watching their equity stagnate won't care that the CEO earned that big bonus by doing X, Y, and Z. All they'll see is a leader reaping rewards while everyone else suffers. It's the board's job to make sure management understands that sacrifice starts at the top. (See Rule #11, "Buy Your Wastebasket at Staples.")

Now, you wouldn't think board members would have to be reminded to be tough. After all, people asked to serve on boards are almost by definition highly successful leaders in their respective fields, and they didn't get to the top by being wallflowers. Yet, when they leave their own domains and enter another company's inner sanctum, many become polite visitors hesitant to assert power for fear of seeming rude or intrusive.

Minow recalls a conversation she had with one director. "I'm always asking the accounting firm to give us numbers in a different format I think would work better. But they never respond," the man told her. "What should I do?"

"*Fire them*," Minow replied.

"No, really, what should I do?"

"Fire them," Minow repeated. "They work for you!"

"In his other life, this man was the hard-charging CEO of his own company. It stunned me that this guy, who in his capacity as CEO was so feisty and fearless…seemed intimidated," says Minow.

By contrast, directors with the tenacity to hold managers to strict performance standards do themselves, the company, shareholders, and even the CEOs themselves, a great service. It's the sort of leadership that takes place behind closed doors and rarely earns public praise, but it just might keep a company's reputation out of the frying pan when activists or reporters embark on the latest roundup of corporations that enriched their managers while impoverishing their shareholders.

——————— Rule No. 24 ———————
Write The Proxy In English
Transparency on Excutive Pay Begins With Clarity

At a time when Congress and government regulators are raising the specter of regulating or capping compensation in the corporate sector, boards face a persistent Catch-22: how do they attract and retain leaders capable of guiding the company through difficult times without drawing the ire of shareholders and the public outraged by real and perceived excesses in CEO compensation?

Pay restraints or caps may attract headlines but, as long as the free market system prevails in the United States, companies will have to pay the compensation necessary to attract and retain qualified leadership, says Pearl Meyer, co-founder and senior managing director of Steven Hall & Partners in New York, and one of the nation's leading consultants on executive compensation.

Meyer, a 2010 inductee into The Directorship Institute's Corporate Governance Hall of Fame, says the current period is, by far, the most contentious she's seen in more than 30 years of advising companies and boards on pay practices. She believes that most of the anger directed at CEO compensation, while fueled by the troubled economy, stems from a fundamental lack of public understanding about just what executives do to earn their paychecks.

"It's easy for the public to understand why Madonna gets paid millions for singing and dancing or Tiger Woods for hitting a golf ball," Meyer says. "But when people look at the individuals running corporations, they see them sitting in big offices and nice automobiles with drivers, or in private corporate aircraft, and they think, 'My God, I can do that.'"

"There is a lack of appreciation and understanding of the quality and value, sacrifices and personal cost of leadership and its responsibilities and the decision making, the years of striving, the expertise, and the personal wisdom and strength required to lead an organization," Meyer says "These are tough jobs and the reason we pay CEOs a lot is that they have unique talents, strengths, and records of success."

According to Meyer, many boards become their own worst public relations enemies by hiding their pay-related methodologies behind closed doors or under reams of financial jargon. They and the companies they serve can no longer afford such lack of clarity. Today's bellicose environment requires absolute transparency in all communications with investors, the press, and the public.

Chiefly, most boards have failed to ensure that the company's potentially most valuable communications tool – the proxy statement – is put to optimum use. Anyone who has spent much time looking through proxies knows that most are repetitive and laden with boilerplate legal terminology and arcane phraseology to a point that they are almost unreadable.

When investors or journalists comb through a proxy statement, they naturally gravitate to one of the few sections of the document that anyone should be able to grasp at once: the bottom-line numbers on how much the top executives earned and for what. The numbers are there (they have to be) but, in the absence of supporting information that is well-reasoned and clearly stated, observers will fill in the blanks themselves, often concluding that the eye-popping salaries, bonuses, and stock grants are the result of cozy arrangements with compliant boards, rather that rewards realistically tied to measurable performance.

The first task, says Meyer, is to take the writing of the

proxy out of the hands of legal counsel and into the hands of the most skilled writers and communicators available. While counsel certainly must guide and review the document, the emphasis should be on making sure everybody can understand it. "To protect themselves and their reputations, boards have to communicate. They have to rewrite their proxies with an executive summary, as well as tables and charts that are not repetitive, not long-winded."

The proxy should make clear precisely the program's architecture and what compensation standards are in place for top management – how salary, annual and long-term incentives, and equity grants were determined.

As scrutiny on corporate pay intensifies, Meyer believes companies will, and should, moderate peripherals such as gross-ups, severance, supplementary benefits, and perquisites. "Peripherals are not linked to performance or the long-term value of the corporation, or to the price of the stock and the welfare of the shareholders or other stakeholders," Meyer says.

She also sees companies moving away from compensation packages that maximize bonuses and minimize base salary. In the past, a salary of, say, $250,000, with $1 million in bonus was viewed as an appropriate way to incentivize creative thinking and reward strong leadership. In a more cautious period, coming off an historic market collapse, such structures are seen in a different light altogether. Says Meyer, "Boards need to make sure that the individual can live on his salary and threshold bonuses without the pressure to earn a large incentive award and take unwarranted risks."

Incentives that a board does implement must be carefully tied to the underlying values and long-term objectives of the corporation – not just a single year's earnings or a temporary spike in stock performance. Companies may benefit from one-time market conditions or other factors having little to do with CEO or other executive performance.

"There's a widespread misunderstanding that CEOs can create or control stock price," Meyer says. "One year, a pharmaceutical company had fabulous operating and stock performance. Its executives were well-rewarded and everybody was pleased with the result. That was 2007. By the time the annual meeting occurred in the spring of 2008, the market had gone down and this company's stock with it. Shareholders complained bitterly about why the executives were so well paid when their stock was down."

By the time those payouts appeared in the 2008 proxy, the good times of 2007 were long forgotten. The whopping payouts to the CEO and other executives for 2007 results echoed like a slap in the face to investors.

Alternatively, consider the company's long-term growth objectives and tie more compensation directly to the achievement of those benchmarks, Meyer suggests. Pay structured in this way not only more closely aligns executive pay with the company's concrete goals, but it's much more readily acceptable to stockholders and understandable to the public as well.

With a sound, transparent pay structure in place, you may not silence every critic, but you will be able to defend those figures with sound and honest reasoning. The proxy is a critical place to start, but don't limit your communication just to the proxy. "Both management and directors should have further dialogue with shareholders," Meyer says. "Use any means you can find to communicate and educate. Directors need to insist on this new approach to reassure stockholders of the soundness of their oversight and protect their reputations, which are at stake."

RULE NO. 25

THE BEST ADVISORS
ASK THE BEST QUESTIONS

If You Don't Get the Answers You Need, Ask Until You Do

At a time when public faith in corporations has been shaken to its foundations, everyone from politicians to shareholders to NGOs is demanding that boards of directors take a more active role in oversight than ever before. That's easy enough to say, but it may be a tall order for board members who are not necessarily experts on the industry in which the company competes.

Directors devote an average of 250 hours per year to each board on which they sit, according to the National Association of Corporate Directors. That's a lot more than the 150 hours they spent a few years back when membership was viewed as more of an honorary position. Yet, even 250 hours are hardly enough to know a company inside and out. Fortunately, boards don't need to have all of the answers in order to serve effectively. What they need are the right questions.

Peter Gleason, the Managing Director and CFO of the National Association of Corporate Directors (NACD), identifies five key questions that any board should ask the chief executive. (If you are a CEO, you should already have answers for these questions. If the board doesn't ask, make them part of the conversation.)

Question 1: Do we have the right leadership team? Hiring a CEO capable of carrying the company's mission forward and inspiring employees is perhaps the single most important function of the board. But personnel oversight doesn't stop there. While CEOs deserve the latitude to surround themselves with managers they trust, the days when boards could passively assume the competency of other C-suite leaders are over.

"You have to be assured that your chief executive has the right team in place to get the job done," Gleason says. He or she should be able to speak persuasively about why each manager is vital to the organization and, if directors believe there are weak links on the team, the board should open a candid dialogue to review those concerns, adds Gleason. Boards should get to know the C-suite leaders in both professional and social settings. As Gleason points out, executive sessions provide an appropriate venue for directors to discuss both the performance of the management team and their own performance at board meetings.

Question 2: Are we strategically aligned? Every company has a strategic plan, but it's worthless if the board does not understand the strategy or isn't satisfied that the goals are both realistic and worthy. "You need to be sure about all of the assumptions made in the plan," Gleason says. "What is management's plan to go from point A to point B? How are they going to get this done? What marketplace assumptions is the plan based on? What are the market barriers?"

Question 3: How are we managing risk? Any company by definition operates in a state of constant risk, from competition to potential crisis. Is your company prepared? Have they determined risk assignments and an appropriate structure for identifying exactly where the risks lie and how they are being evaluated and handled."

In today's business and media environment, even acceptable risk can lead directly to a public crisis. It is imperative for you to know exactly what sort of crisis team the company has in place, who's on it, how quickly they can respond in an emergency, what steps they will take, and, vitally, how you as the board will interact with them in the event of a crisis.

Make sure that the crisis team isn't just a list of names, but that its members meet and drill periodically. The next crisis you face will not be the one you expected, which is why the team must be comfortable enough with their procedures to respond to just about anything.

Question 4: What is our information flow? Communications has two components, internal and external. "It's vital that the information channels are open, both from the management team to the board, and from the management team to the public," Gleason says. Be certain that managers can detail how these channels operate both on a daily basis and during emergencies so that you get all of the information you need in a timely manner.

In an age when a small headache can become a life-threatening crisis, it is absolutely essential that your company has a strong, integrated strategy for using the social media such as blogs, YouTube, Twitter, and Facebook. Make sure that your CEO has a working knowledge of the social media and the right team in place to monitor what is said about the company online. Where appropriate, actively use the social media to reach out to the public and tell the company's story.

Question 5: Are we ethical? Take nothing for granted and do not be satisfied with generalities, or you may find yourself personally exposed as a director of the latest WorldCom or Enron. Ask your CEO precisely what ethical standards he or she has set for the company and, just as important, how those standards are passed down through the ranks to every employee. "If you see any lapse, you as the board need to act," Gleason says.

If you don't like the answers, ask again, and keep asking until you are fully satisfied, Gleason advises. "You have to make it clear that you have high standards and you will hold yourselves and the company accountable to them."

Rule No. 26
The Boardroom is Not a Blackberry Patch

*Peacetime Performance
Dictates Crisis Effectiveness*

During board meetings, the CEO of one company made a habit of checking his Blackberry every couple of minutes. He probably thought he was making the most of his time. After all, one of the signature abilities of any business leader is juggling multiple tasks without letting anything crash. Yet, with that seemingly innocuous habit, the CEO was unwittingly putting his entire company at risk.

When a crisis occurs, any corporation naturally looks to its board for wisdom, a shared sense of purpose, and strong, firm advice. A board's guidance can make or break a company facing a life-threatening emergency. But just as a football team can't start learning its plays during the Super Bowl, a board of directors cannot be expected to find its shared identity and purpose after a crisis has already begun. The qualities that define your board are shaped during peacetime, through many small acts that collectively reinforce or undermine its ability to be effective in times of need.

In the case of that wild-sprouting Blackberry, the CEO's discreet peeks were quickly interpreted by board members as license to take care of their own outside business instead of the business at hand. Implicitly, "every director had permission to check their Blackberries. Then, every senior executive present said, 'OK, those are the standards,'" recalls Stuart R. Levine, who was a director for the company. "The board sets the tone at the top of an organization, so I can only imagine what kinds of behaviors were being duplicated throughout the company."

As Levine points out, checking your messages amid a meeting "is a classic way of telling people, 'what you're saying is important to me – *sort of.*'"

In addition to serving on many boards himself, Levine is founder and CEO of Stuart Levine & Associates LLC, which helps international companies on issues such as governance, leadership, and organizational effectiveness. A former CEO of Dale Carnegie & Associates Inc., Levine is author of *The Six Fundamentals of Success* and *Cut to the Chase*, emphasizing the crucial role that organization and time management play in corporate governance.

Attention to the mundane details, and to the logistics and processes that pertain to every board-related event, has enormous impact on how boards function during crises and stressful periods. "There will be a time in the life of every corporation when there is a crisis," says Levine. "The fundamental principle in life and business success is respectful relationships. Respectful relationships are tethered to how we function together around that boardroom table."

These crucial details include:

Start on time. A meeting or phone conference scheduled for 8:30 a.m. starts at 8:30, whether everyone has arrived or not. Promptness may seem like a common courtesy, but there's a more important dynamic at work. Routinely waiting 15 or 20 minutes for everyone to show up subtly and insidiously divides your board into two camps – those who arrive on time and those who don't. The former will resent the latter, and you've needlessly created factions in place of the unity that is your goal.

Starting on time sets a tone of seriousness and focus, and stragglers will quickly get the message that punctuality is expected of them. Once the meeting starts, it should also proceed according to a clearly established agenda and end on time, Levine says. If you are leading the discussion, it's up to you to keep the conversation on point and gently, but clearly, reign in board members who stray from the topics at hand.

Insist that everyone contributes. Most of us remember certain high school classes in which one or two vocal students were allowed to dominate class discussions. Even distinguished boards are susceptible to the same dynamic. Just as a good teacher encourages broad classroom participation, good board leaders must insist on hearing from everybody.

"In most successful boards I've been on, the chair or whoever's leading the conversation that day will go around the table asking for your input on every decision," Levine says.

Obviously, silent members deny the company their potentially valuable insights. Importantly too, people who don't speak up are less likely to take personal ownership of group decisions, which can be fatal during a crisis when you need every member to feel fully vested in the board's mission.

When a crisis occurs, "People will say, 'I never heard this,' or 'Why wasn't that discussed?' In truth, it was discussed. They just didn't hear it because they weren't really participating. They were there physically, but no one challenged them to verbalize an opinion," Levine says.

Provide the right advance information. E-mail technology makes it possible to transmit an almost unlimited quantity of reports and other information. But quantity isn't quality, Levine says. As a board leader, insist that corporate officers carefully vet and cull materials in advance to ensure that directors get what they need in order to make decisions, without overwhelming them with massive information. Materials should be sent five or six days before the meeting.

As a corollary, encourage officers to keep their presentations at the meetings concise. Avoid lengthy PowerPoint presentations that rehash what was in the mailed packet. Assume instead that directors have read and digested the material and use the in-person presentation to highlight specific areas of concern or answer their questions.

In a crisis, proper use of directors' time only becomes more important. Make sure that directors are briefed individually and given pertinent documents before you meet in person to discuss the crisis, Levine advises. When you do meet, directors will then be able to directly offer crucial advice rather than expend precious time on the basics of the situation.

Plan the right dinner. Most companies hold a dinner for board members and top executives the night before a meeting to allow for informal conversations in a relaxed environment. It is a great opportunity for team building, but only if the setting fosters discussion of the issues facing the company.

"One board I was on held the dinner in a noisy restaurant," Levine recalls. The group naturally divided up into smaller conversations, since that was the only way they could speak privately. "You've effectively divided the board," he says. By contrast, Levine is currently on a board that meets in a private dining room. "We can hear each other and have an intelligent discussion about strategic issues," he says. "And the door is closed, so there's no question of breach of confidence."

Such matters may seem trivial compared with the weighty issues facing large companies, and board leaders may be reluctant to impose clear-cut rules of conduct on members who are clearly distinguished, accomplished professionals. Yet boards, if anything, require even greater attention to basic structures and meeting etiquette, Levine insists, since they only meet face-to-face a few times each year and are charged with ever-greater oversight of the companies they serve.

"Utilization of time and energy and brain power becomes incredibly important," he says. "There is only so much oxygen in any particular room, so developing clear agendas in a board meeting, and adhering to them, becomes crucial."

Each shrewd logistical step helps transform a board from a loose affiliation of distinguished persons into a unified force ready to act in the company's best interest, both in peacetime and during crises.

SECTION SIX

Leadership in the Digital Era

A lot has changed in 28 years. Johnson & Johnson, whose fabled response to poisoned Tylenol bottles in 1982 provided an invaluable playbook for how to behave during a corporate emergency, came under fire in early 2010 amid a recall of several products, including Tylenol, due to a musty, mildewing aroma in packages. In January, the Food and Drug Administration delivered a stinging, highly public rebuke of the company for its slow response after customer complaints first surfaced.

Even after the FDA's action, Johnson & Johnson's response seemed decidedly muted: by mid-February, recall information was tucked away in the "News" section of the J&J website, which linked visitors to another site offering factual information but little in the way of personal communication that might put the story in context for millions of loyal customers.

Bloggers and journalists, taking cues from the FDA, quickly filled the vacuum. "Consumers must work through the fine print to get the information they need," one pharmaceutical blogger complained. A *New York Times* headline intoned, "In Recall, A Role Model Stumbles." And a reporter for *The Christian Science Monitor* pointed out that the "sad" episode served as "a reminder of how fragile corporate reputations are."

It's important to note that the 1982 crisis was much more severe in that people actually died. In 2010, the most serious physical effects appeared to be mild, temporary gastrointestinal disturbances. Yet two conclusions seem inescapable: first, the master forgot its own lessons in crisis management and, second, different times demand different actions.

In 1982, corporations functioned in a communications world that was, by and large, *linear*. In the wake of an accident, crime, or other unexpected event, a corporate communications team fielded calls from a predictable array of trade, business, and mainstream print media. If the story had good visuals, they spoke to television producers as well.

Each of those entities operated with rigid, predictable news cycles that were well understood by reporters and public relations executives alike. Cable television was in its infancy, and computer scientists were still developing fundamental protocols for something that would come to be called the Internet.

In this linear world, bad press might inspire activist groups to picket your offices. In turn, politicians, sensing a photo op or two, would demand answers and promise new regulations. Life wasn't easy, but controlling your message wasn't that hard if you maintained good trusting relations with a handful of powerful gatekeepers among the press, grassroots operatives, elected officials, and regulators.

Today, the linear model has been replaced by a circle with you, the corporation, sitting in the middle and vulnerable to attack at any time from any direction, without warning. The old media gatekeepers are struggling just to survive, and they no longer drive news cycles. Actually, the term "news cycle" is meaningless. In its place there's a vast, amorphous, unpredictable population blogging or Twittering away on laptops, PCs, and Blackberries.

Who are these people? The 2009 State of the Blogosphere report by Technorati discredits any stereotypes about bloggers as scruffy post-adolescents with too much time on their hands. The report found:

- 70 percent of bloggers have college degrees.
- 40 percent have a household income above $75,000.
- 28 percent are professionals (either paid to blog or blogging for work) and, of those, *40 percent are journalists.*

The Internet has resulted in a breathtaking democratization of information, and cell phone cameras have created a limitless army of impromptu photojournalists poised to capture anything in real time from an airline disaster to a Congressional slip of the tongue. People no longer passively await the arrival of the newspaper or the six o'clock news. They want – they demand! – the right to be part of the story, to speak their minds.

Voices from the blogosphere may be legitimate and responsible or thoroughly reckless. The fact is, you don't know who will be saying what about your company. Any of these voices can, and will, comment thoughtfully or irresponsibly on your company as damaging reports, accurate or not, go viral in a flash.

Consider the case of Domino's pizza. In April 2009, a pair of Domino's workers in North Carolina narrated a video of themselves doing disgusting things to food before sending it out the door. They then posted the videos on the world's most popular video-sharing website, YouTube. When word of the video reached Domino's headquarters, executives did all the right things…*according to the old, linear model.* They fired the workers, called in the local health department, discarded food at the branch where the pranksters worked, prepared an open, forthright response for the mainstream press, and waited for the crisis to pass.

In 1982, the story would have died down. Even if the pranksters had somehow managed to produce a video in those pre-cell phone days, it would have found brief air time or, more likely, none at all. Unlike the Tylenol case, it was a prank that resulted in some queasy stomachs, perhaps, but no injuries. Good relations with responsible TV gatekeepers would have buried the video.

By 2009 standards, however, Domino's had already put its brand at terrible risk before the crisis erupted, by having to be alerted to the video by somebody outside the company. They should have known within moments of when it first appeared. They should have been monitoring YouTube and other outlets for mentions of their brand. Consider that more than 100 million people go to YouTube every month and that 24 hours of new video are uploaded every minute. With that sort of access to viewers, just about anyone can hijack your brand without warning.

Instead, the Domino's old-style crisis response system plodded forward like a trusty plow horse, the story spread wildly on the Web. Within two days, the video was viewed more than a million times on YouTube. Google searches for Domino's revealed multiple first-page listings for the video, and Twitter was buzzing. Meanwhile, executives at Domino's were flat-footedly creating their own YouTube video and Twitter account to respond to the crisis days after two minimum wage pizza workers had hijacked the billion dollar brand. But the damage was largely done. The mainstream press, rather than driving the story, was reduced to commenting on how new media drove it.

A *New York Times* headline on April 16 said it all: "Video Prank at Domino's Taints Brand." An opinion polling company called YouGov (online and instantaneous, of course) reported that, in the space of two days, consumer impressions of Domino's had gone from positive to negative. Domino's spokesman Tim McIntire told the paper, "We got blindsided by two idiots with a video camera and an awful idea." More accurately, the company was blindsided by forces far more ominous and powerful. The game has changed forever.

Corporations, by the way, aren't the only ones that get stung when they overlook or mismanage the new game. President Obama is rightly referred to as the first Internet president because of the savvy he and his staff demonstrated during his campaign in amassing legions of supporters and donors online. Yet the White House showed no such savvy after staffers approved a publicity photo shoot of Air Force One flying low over the Statue of Liberty in New York.

When the White House press corps pushed spokesman Robert Gibbs, he reverted to a time-honored strategy for preventing potentially embarrassing stories from gaining steam: he promised to look into it and get back to them. Unfortunately, homemade videos were already flooding websites with images of the huge jet, flanked by a pair of fighter planes, screaming over lower Manhattan, and of terrified New Yorkers fleeing their offices in fear of a 9/11 repeat. The incident would have been embarrassing in any case, but the sluggish response from a White House press office seemingly oblivious to the potentially damaging powers of instant communications exacerbated an early embarrassment for the Obama presidency.

The good news is that the same forces that threaten to

overwhelm the unprepared also present great opportunities for those who are willing to engage the new world on its own terms. Americans do not demand perfection, but they do demand action. In the following chapters, we'll look at a variety of corporate responses and actions in the new social media space, some forward-thinking and others disastrously retro.

In any event, companies are learning. It's safe to say that Domino's is already creating a template for more effective crisis management in the digital era. If they get blindsided again, whose fault will that be?

—— RULE No. 27 ——

GET IN THE GAME

The Conversations That Make or Break Your Brand Occur in the Blogs With or Without You

---

When it comes to corporations using the social media to the fullest and most positive extent, there may be nobody who does it better than Southwest Airlines.

Between spring 2008 and spring 2009, Southwest logged more than two million unique visitors to its blog, "Nuts about Southwest" (a play on the airline's no-frills, peanuts-only policy). Note that the blog is completely distinct from the airline's sales-oriented website. You can link to that site if you want fares or tickets, but that's not the purpose of the blog.

"People have made it known very clearly that they don't go into these social media tools to be sold products and services," says Linda Rutherford, Southwest's Vice President of Communications and Strategic Outreach. In other words, *social media platforms are about protecting and enhancing your brand, not marketing.* The idea is to start a dialogue with customers, manage the brand, develop a well of goodwill, and, when necessary, deal effectively with crises.

Southwest didn't just leap into the social media space with a top-down approach. They started by listening. "We identified 75 or 80 sites that were talking about Southwest," Rutherford says. "After monitoring them, we were able to determine who the aviation nuts were, who the airplane geeks were, who the people were who closely watch our business. We could tell where our employees were spending their time putting up blog posts. We knew what kinds of conversations were happening, and where."

First launched in 2006, Nuts about Southwest was completely upgraded in early 2008. Today the site includes video blogs, a Flickr feed, a news section, instant polling, and a weekly podcast, among other features. The blog features regular posts from about 40 employees, including top managers. But any member of the public who wants to contribute need only register.

Passengers post their own photos of Southwest planes, stories about fun trips they've taken, or trivia about operations or aircraft. Inevitably, too, some use the space to vent. "Sometimes, executives see things on the blog that have a lot of passion and the passion isn't, 'I love you, Southwest.' It's more like, 'I'm angry at you. Why did you do this?'

"And, they wonder, how's this a good thing?" Rutherford continues. "Why do we have this type of criticism? What they don't understand is that people would be saying those things anyway. But they're saying them on our forum with an opportunity for us to weigh in."

While Southwest does set certain guidelines about language and civility, posters who respect the rules are free to share the good, the bad, and the ugly. It helps that, since its founding in

1971, Southwest has developed a corporate identity of plain talk and direct outreach to customers. "We've always had a reputation for telling it exactly like it is. We're known as a brand that, when the industry zigs, we zag," says Rutherford. "We do things a little differently."

Still, the natural desire to control the message is a strong one. "Every now and then we have to remind [executives] that we no longer live in a command and control world," Rutherford says. When one asked her recently to delete a derogatory post, Rutherford declined, explaining, "We would lose all credibility." More often than not, angry posts "self-correct," she says, as loyal customers leap to the airline's defense. "We can sit back and let people have that conversation. That's exactly what it's meant to be."

Users also become a valuable resource in helping guide customer service decisions. In 2007, when Southwest considered dropping its trademark choice-based seating as a way to woo business travelers, CEO Gary Kelly asked bloggers how they'd feel about assigned seats. In no time, 700 impassioned responses told Kelly in no uncertain terms that they hated the idea. Choosing your seat on Southwest was something passengers could still control, they said, and it was one of the reasons they selected Southwest over other airlines.

"We were able to get some great insights that matched what we were getting [when] we talked to passengers at the airport," Rutherford says. "It was an inexpensive way to validate what we were hearing, which was, 'don't assign seats but do come up with a new way to board the aircraft.' And that's what we did."

As such, paying attention to social media voices helped the airline avoid a decision that could have seriously impaired its brand.

All airlines must plan for the unthinkable, and Southwest

has fully incorporated the social media into its plans in the event of a crash. As of this writing, Southwest has had no such incident since 2005, before the airline became involved in the social media. Today, Southwest has incorporated a "dark site" onto its blog. In the event of an accident, people entering the blog would automatically be sent to the dark site, confirming the accident and any other verified details, such as the number of passengers, and where the plane crashed.

"At the same time that we post to employees and news media, we would post the exact same information, once it's been approved by our emergency director, to our blog, and to Twitter and Facebook," Rutherford says. "It's written into the plan so that all the channels have the communications to be fully transparent. That's why you plan for these things."

Rule No. 28

Social Media are the Media

It's Corporate Malpractice to Ignore the Online Conversation

One day not long ago, a top company in the amusement industry was advised of a forthcoming story in a leading national newspaper that would highlight disappointing financial results, calling into question the future of the company and even the industry itself.

Before the advent of blogs and other social media, the predictable corporate response may have been to lie low, hope the article didn't cause too many waves, and downplay the story with reporters who called for follow-ups. Maybe then such discretion would have been, proverbially, the better part of valor. Yet even then, such a strategy risked ceding control of the story to the media and trapping the company in a vulnerable defensive position.

Today's digital world increases that risk exponentially and, in so many cases, a defensive posture is the riskiest of all. Fortunately, the company we're thinking of took a very different approach. Armed with detailed information on all the bloggers covering its industry, with intelligence on which ones had already written about the company itself in a neutral or positive light, the company went on the offense with a concerted social media plan. A wise decision in light of research proving that, collectively, the bloggers had a readership many times that of the newspaper.

The day before the negative story appeared, the company sent each important blogger a personal note along with a link to a recent television interview in which the CEO, an articulate, confident leader, laid out a clear, persuasive case for why the company would surmount the difficult economic times ahead.

There was no mention of the bad news to come the next day. However, by the time that story ran, the blogs had been posting the positive message for nearly 24-hours, effectively neutralizing most of the damage among those readers who follow the industry most carefully. On the morning the news appeared, the chief executive made himself available to more than a dozen key bloggers for an online roundtable discussion. The bloggers were able to ask frank questions and get straight, unfiltered responses. The forthrightness paid off in respectful coverage. Note that this type of strategy could only come after careful preparation. You cannot use the social media to respond to a crisis at the same time that you are trying to figure out how the social media work.

This preparation starts with listening carefully. The 118 million blogs currently being tracked online today make an awful lot of noise. The ones that require your closest attention are the 20, 50, or, in some cases, 150 dedicated bloggers who post regularly about you and your industry.

But blogs are only a part of the social media. Monitor Twitter to keep track of the latest Tweets that could go viral and impact your brand. Have someone trolling YouTube so the next video slamming your industry or brand doesn't catch you off guard. Only by listening can you put yourself ahead of the curve with responses that make you look confident and strong rather than weak and defensive.

Don't form a committee to explore your options; don't assign your Senior VP for Strategy to look into it when he gets back from vacation. Tell your savviest Web marketers they're switching from sales to brand protection. The fact is, most marketing people are so focused on using these technologies to ramp up sales and market share that they aren't watching the back door. Make it their job to keep track of anything that's said, good or bad, about your company, and to keep you informed. If they're too drilled in promotional palaver to make the transformation, find someone else who can. Survey your employees to find out what they've been doing in the online space. Chances are, you already have several passionate, media-savvy employees just waiting to be unleashed to support the brand.

Why such aggressive steps? Because *failure to develop a social media strategy to protect your brand from assaults is tantamount to corporate malpractice.*

During the height of the financial crisis of late 2008, one financial services firm was getting pummeled on a daily basis by a prominent liberal-leaning blog. Now, this company was mired in tradition, and its corporate communications strategy revolved solely around periodic conversations with *The Wall*

Street Journal or beat business reporters from the largest daily newspapers and wires. The company did not understand blogging, and did not want to. Yet the more it tried to ignore these detractors, the more vehement and conspicuous they became. Far from an obscure online crank, this blog loomed large on the daily reading list of almost every aide in the White House and on Capitol Hill, Republican or Democratic.

Furthermore, the blog, while undeniably slanted to a particular viewpoint, wasn't just tossing bombs. It was raising serious, legitimate questions.

Outside advisors finally convinced the company to reach out to the bloggers. Its media director first sent a friendly, professional email explaining the company's positions and responding to some of the more inflammatory charges. The company was shocked to see its message posted, word-for-word, along with a respectful note from the bloggers.

Encouraged, the company offered up a senior executive to respond directly to questions.

We'd love to say that the ensuing dialogue turned the blog and its readership from haters into lovers. Of course, that didn't happen. Hardened perceptions cannot be transformed by sudden niceties, especially when those perceptions are supported by facts. But the choice is yours. Will you let the problem sit and fester or will you seize the day and claim equal time to advance your position? You can win respect just by being willing to join the fray, and that respect may be capital in the bank for the next media embattlement. In this case, the overall tone did become markedly more civil. At least the company was assured of having its own voice heard as it had taken a major step toward controlling its own message.

If nothing else, it was no longer committing corporate malpractice.

Rule No. 29

Social Media are the CEO's 21st Century Telephone

In the Online Space, You Get to Tell Your Company's Story and Your Own

---

If you run a company and are still wondering whether to personally dive into the social media space, consider the words of a chief executive in Boston named Paul Levy: "A CEO not having a blog today is like a CEO 20 years ago not using a telephone."

Levy is no 20-something running a digital startup out of a converted warehouse, but the 50-something head of Beth Israel Deaconess Medical Center, a major Harvard teaching hospital with roots stretching back to the late 19th century.

"If part of your job as CEO is to represent your organization in the public eye in a way that is consistent with your strategic objectives…why would you not use new methods like blogs, Facebook, and Twitter, which are effective in their own way in carrying out that function?" he asks.

Levy launched his blog in 2006, after reading an article about some Fortune 500 CEOs who were doing the same. "I thought, gee, I have a really interesting job, I'm not a Fortune 500 president, but I'm the CEO of a pretty important hospital. Why don't I give it a try and see what happens?"

Since then, "Running a Hospital" has become an indispensible tool. Not only does it give him a platform for sharing his views on hospitals, medicine, and the forces shaping his industry, but it is actively helping him to guide the storied Beth Israel Deaconess through some of the most difficult economic times in memory.

He was particularly intrigued by the chance to communicate his thoughts directly to the public without conforming to the editorial mandates of a traditional media gatekeeper. It was "like writing op-eds without being filtered," he says. "I just thought that what goes on in the hospital and medical world is of tremendous public interest.... If I could write about it in an interesting way, it might be useful or entertaining to people to learn about it."

"Running a Hospital" includes a mixture of hospital news, information on medical breakthroughs and policies, and personal musings, as well as links to a host of medical and other sites Levy finds interesting.

Readership, slow at first, took off after an article in the *Boston Globe* in October 2006 described Levy's initiative. From 31,000 visitors in the fourth quarter of 2006, the blog has grown to reach hundreds of thousands of readers in 2009.

Since he conceived the blog as a way to communicate with the outside world, what has surprised Levy most has been its usefulness in encouraging excellence among the center's 5,000-plus employees, who range from cafeteria cooks and custodians to some of the world's most renowned clinicians.

"I started writing stories about some of our quality and safety improvements here, and publishing the clinical outcomes," he says. "I think the first ones were about central line infections. It was at that point that I discovered the blog as a management tool, because, when I would publish things about what people were doing here that were good, they would feel proud and it was motivational. But also because they knew I would be writing about what they were doing, I think it made them more attentive and gave them a greater impetus to do better than they might have otherwise."

Levy is quick to note that the blog doesn't answer every

communications need. For example, when the center faced a financial crisis forcing cutbacks, Levy emailed all employees directly, detailing the challenges. Though he later posted the same information on his blog, emailing was the only way to ensure that everyone would see the numbers. "And, if I want to engage people on the staff to talk about a certain issue, we create an in-house chat room where people can do that," he adds.

Another caveat: keep in mind that direct, instant communication without filters means there's nobody to catch errors or misstatements. "Once it's out there, it's out there," Levy says. "The antidote to that is, you can correct it quickly, too. If I print something on the blog that's wrong and someone writes to me immediately and says you really messed up on that, I can fix it."

Levy recalls one post he wrote, which was about a new asthma treatment he found particularly fascinating. A reader pointed out that the hospital had a commercial relationship with the company doing the trials, suggesting Levy's post was less than disinterested. "I didn't know that when I wrote the thing," Levy recalls. "So I added an addendum to the post. I said, 'It has come to my attention that we have a commercial relationship with the company engaged in the trials. I was not aware of this before today and I apologize for mentioning it in my original post.'

"End of story. What could have been, in a different venue, an embarrassing, long-lived story, basically in this case, was over."

—————————— **RULE No. 30** ——————————

YOU WILL BE DISCOVERED

*Why the Internet is More
Like Walking Than Driving*

In 2008, a senior executive for Burger King took an unusual (and ultimately disastrous) tack during a 2008 labor dispute with union leaders over the farm workers who were picking vegetables for the chain. In addition to whatever public statements the company made, this executive started posting disparaging online comments about labor leaders and their practices – using his daughter's screen name.

The idea must have seemed so clever, so…safe. Who would ever find out?

Now, it's highly unlikely that this executive would have ever dreamed of a similarly phony campaign on paper via traditional media. Imagine giving a false name to a reporter, or trying to pose as someone you're not – while appearing in a television news interview.

Yet the Internet sometimes encourages an anything-goes dynamic. Check out a journalistic website and the comments beneath any random news item. You'll see how quickly people abandon personal rules of civility, decorum, and restraint when they think they're invisible. Words fly from their fingers that would never cross their lips at a neighborhood barbecue.

Amid the profusion of verbal missiles fired under the alias of someone's pet schnauzer or favorite *Star Wars* character, the Burger King executive may not have even considered his ploy unethical. The Internet feels like driving, but it is really walking. We motor along in the cocoon of our cars, occasionally feeling frustrated enough to treat others with disdain. By contrast, imagine tailgating or yelling (the equivalent of honking) at a slow walker. It would embarrass and possibly put us in harm's way.

Burger King paid a high price for its lesson in digital circumspection. Inevitably, some computer experts traced the comments back to the executive, and a Florida newspaper broke the story. The executive was fired, and Burger King's CEO made a public apology for this incident, which endangered the company's brand simply by making the company look devious and petty.

Burger King is by no means the only corporate ship to have scraped its hull on the shoals of the blogosphere. On his "Web Strategy" blog, www.businessinsider.com, social media expert Jeremiah Owyang keeps a running list of "Brands that Got Punk'd by Social Media." The list includes some of the most recognizable names in corporate America. While most companies stumble their way onto the list through honest goofs rather than devious schemes, virtually every case starts with somebody underestimating the power and the seriousness of the social media.

We cannot say this emphatically enough: *do not play around on the Internet*. Always use your own name and title and treat every missive, however casual, as though you were writing for posterity, and for the close scrutiny of friend and foe alike. Executives who anonymously goad an adversary or, conversely, plant false testimonials on their own behalf risk creating problems far greater than whatever issue prompted their participation in the first place. Memorize four simple words from Richard Jalichandra, the CEO of Technorati and today's most important authority on blogs: "You will be discovered."

Jalichandra faced a similar temptation of his own shortly after joining the company in October 2007. An influential technology writer began using his own blog to sharply criticize Jalichandra, implying that he never should have become CEO.

"We'd never met before, he didn't know me, and he absolutely flamed me," Jalichandra recalls. Within a short while, blog responders started piling on. It was open season on Richard Jalichandra, and his seat at Technorati was barely warm!

Naturally enough, Jalichandra was tempted to salve his ego by sending that blog a few choice insults of his own under an assumed name. Had he chosen that course, he might have joined the Burger King executive in search of a new job. Instead, he played it straight, posting a response under his own name and title. "I said, 'I actually have a pretty good track record. Why don't you give me six months before you throw me in the garbage can?' The stream of comments after that were 70-80 percent in my favor," he recalls. The general tenor was now, *give the guy a chance.*

"When you actually engage them, people are like, 'Wow, you're brave enough to step into this? – I'll at least give you one chance and listen to you.'"

Even the blogger was conciliatory and eventually became a friendly acquaintance after realizing Jalichandra was open to discuss breaking stories (and did so several times thereafter). "On one of our first conversations, he said, 'it's a good thing you didn't try to do that anonymously.'"

As Jalichandra adds, "Trust me, they'll figure it out."

SECTION SEVEN

LITIGATION COMMUNICATIONS
Refining an Art in the New Environment

The first challenge of "litigation communications" is to define it, particularly since the concept is susceptible to pernicious misinterpretation and misapplication. First, it is imperative to understand what litigation communications, as we talk about it, does *not* entail. It is not a grab-bag of tricks and spin to glibly obfuscate facts and issues. It is not a practicum to frustrate the opposition with maneuvers in courts of law or the Court of Public Opinion and thereby win a victory by attrition, or exclude the press and the public from learning the truth about a sensitive situation. In many cases, they're going to find it out anyway.

In fact, litigation communications entail the precise opposite. To every extent permitted by the adjudicators, effective litigation communications is all about clarity, openness, and honesty. It is driven by the same intent and style as effective communications at any other level of the corporation and, sometimes, more so.

As such, litigation communications as a leadership art requires its own separate treatment and discussion. In a litigious environment where millions or even billions of dollars, as well as the company's good name, may be at stake, those you're depending on to defend your brand – whether inside counsel, outside counsel, public relations advisors, IR advisors, supportive third parties, or C-suite spokespersons – have very specific leadership tasks and responsibilities even before the first brief is filed, as well as in the aftermath of victory, defeat, or settlement.

Everyone wants to win, especially when the stakes are highest. But victories in court can be Pyrrhic if they irreparably damage the brand. Conversely, ill-advised public declarations and representations can create unwanted legal exposure.

At some point, even the best-run companies and the most committed corporate good citizens can assume they'll be sued by customers, competitors, or the government. At the end of the day, the yardstick of success is not just the outcome of the case or its settlement terms. The long-term impact is the dispositive measure, and that impact is determined by multiple millions of jurors in every venue where the company does business.

— RULE No. 31 —

IN A DIGITAL WORLD, YOU CAN'T JUST TELL YOUR STORY IN COURT

Litigating in a Fishbowl

To the extent that there ever was true separation between events in court and the world outside, those walls have been largely torn down. The Internet and, in particular, blogs have rendered the old notion of keeping courtroom information "out of the papers" seem rather quaint.

In just the past five years or so, newspapers and television have, perforce, relinquished their role in determining what news emerges or does not emerge during corporate litigation. The dozen or so bloggers who follow your industry are the ones who will uncover the details and put them out for the world to see. "They're the ones feeding the mainstream media," says Charles L. "Chip" Babcock, a nationally recognized litigator with Jackson Walker LLP in Dallas.

Combine the blogs with Twitter, Facebook, YouTube, and all other Web-based social media, with their potential to spread information virally and instantaneously, and you'll understand why Babcock believes every company should have a litigation communications team in place and ready to go, in the same way oil companies have disaster response teams prepared for the inevitable spills.

Your team should include outside counsel, in-house counsel, outside crisis communication specialists, and your corporate communications chief, Babcock says. Begin with the assumption that you *will* be sued, that the case *will* draw media interest, and then make sure you team knows exactly how it will respond.

In an age of high-stakes litigation and instant communication, the margin for error is razor thin, and the risks to your brand are incalculable. Among its fundamental tasks, a litigation communications team must:

Speak with one voice. "If you have multiple people speaking, unless they are really tightly coordinated – which never happens – then you're going to be mixing your messages," Babcock says. "From a litigation perspective, you might have somebody in a company saying something that is off message, not true, or ill-informed. That will come back and haunt you during litigation."

Who the spokespersons should be depends, of course, on the size and nature of the crisis and the individual skills of the team members.

Bridge the no comment/comment gap. Lawyers and companies being sued often clam up for fear of angering the judge or having their words used against them in court. Yet, common recourse to "no comment" was self-defeating even in the days when a handful of gatekeeper reporters from the newswires or the local newspapers reigned supreme. Today, "no-comment" is an invitation for the entire world to fill in the blanks. "It can be perceived as an arrogant, unhelpful response and might imply that you couldn't care less about this [lawsuit], as in 'Go away, don't bother us,'" says Babcock.

If you truly can't comment on a crisis because you don't yet have solid facts, provide a placeholder quote, something to the effect of, "We are investigating this matter and will respond in detail when the investigation is complete." In practical terms, that's a comment that a blogger can plug into a story, and it will at least show "that you're not blowing this off," Babcock says.

When you do have facts and are ready to comment, be sure that your message is carefully thought out. Elsewhere in this book, we discuss the importance of openness and honesty, and the advisability of full apologies, if warranted. But openness does not mean shooting off at the mouth with unguarded, unconsidered pronouncements.

Babcock recalls a recent case in which several companies were being sued following an accident that cost many lives.

"My client followed the protocol we had set out: we had one spokesman, and we made no comments until we knew what we were talking about," he says. "We had help from a very strong regional [crisis communications] company, and a disciplined approach.

"Another defendant in the case did not take that approach. The manager of the local office started talking to the press a lot, and he was saying things without counsel or regard to the legal consequences…and a lot of things that were not, in the end, true. His comments found their way into the plaintiff papers a year or two years later and were used against his company…. Their legal position was compromised."

Know when to play defense. Understanding the media during litigation isn't only about getting your own message out. A disciplined team must also be carefully monitoring the media for signs of the opposition's strategy. "If you're monitoring the blogosphere and traditional media, you'll see some of the same themes and words being used repeatedly," advises Babcock. "You'll see documents surfacing that could only come from one source: the lawyers on the other side."

"If there are confidential documents that have been exchanged during discovery and you think the other side is releasing those documents to the press, you can talk to the judge about that," Babcock advises. "If there are comments being made by the plaintiffs' lawyers, you can sometimes use those against them with the court. If the court is irritated by what is being said…that can put a damper on your opponent's willingness to speak in inflammatory, derogatory terms."

Even if the opposition's media tactics cannot be so challenged, you can discern vital elements of their strategy by keeping a close eye on the blogosphere, Babcock says. "It gives you a chance to think if there's a way to counteract the bad publicity that's coming at you."

Know when to go on the offense. A media assault on the opposition before, or during, litigation can easily backfire if it makes you look as if you are attacking or belittling someone who has been victimized by a company mistake.

On the other hand, if you believe you have been wronged by your opposition, a very pointed media campaign may be called for. The classic case was when General Motors sued

NBC over a report on exploding gas tanks in GM trucks. The automaker staged a satellite press conference to expose how NBC had used explosives to detonate the tanks for video purposes, without telling viewers. GM's tactic was potentially risky, as the company might have been depicted as blaming the messenger for disclosing a serious safety problem. But the evidence was solid. NBC apologized and paid GM's legal bills for the case.

Ensure that outside counsel is media savvy. Of all the members of your litigation communications team, your outside counsel may be the last one to fully grasp the importance of a concerted media strategy, Babcock says. "Very few outside counsel understand the public perception phenomenon. It's not something you take a course on in law school, and it runs counter to the setup of the legal system.

"The whole nature of their business is counterintuitive to the fact that a company's public message about a legal problem is every bit as important as what happens at the courthouse," Babcock says. "If the public, as expressed through the bloggers and the mainstream media, get where you're coming from, and understand it, then that can have all sorts of positive effects on what you are trying to do in the courthouse."

RULE No. 32

SOME VICTORIES KILL YOU

*Leadership in Litigation Defines
What Winning Really Means*

Litigation is, of course, an adversarial pursuit. Corporations pay millions of dollars each year to inside and outside counsel to protect their interests with absolute toughness and legal precision. They pay them to win.

Without strong guidance and communication from top leadership, however, a company's drive to prevail in legal disputes against other companies can easily translate into endless, costly, and mutually destructive conflicts in which the original goal (e.g., some important, tangible business objective) becomes lost in the fog of war. As CEO, you can't micromanage every legal maneuver. What you can and must do is make sure that your long-term objectives are clearly articulated and understood by your in-house counsel, hired attorneys, and any of your managers or employees involved in the case. In the best situation, you will also make your objectives known to your opponent and do your best to understand *their* objectives, for frequently their success is tied to yours.

"An attitude set by the corporate leadership that is gladiatorial, with disdain for adversaries, will naturally tend to filter into the litigation and arbitration hearing room," says Walter Gans, a former corporate general counsel and currently a leading arbitration judge. An aggressive corporate culture may serve some purposes very well, but leaders of such companies must be especially adept at channeling it properly.

Otherwise, they risk falling into the sort of nightmare trap that evolved during a recent dispute between a major communications company and one of its primary suppliers, over allegedly defective equipment. At first, the two companies and their leaders seemed genuinely interested in a swift, reasonable resolution. They decided to use professional arbitrators instead of the judicial system. Their decision was hardly unique. Corporations increasingly turn to arbitration to resolve civil suits without the costs, delays, and negative publicity of court actions. Although the decisions are legally binding, disputants have significant latitude in setting the ground rules for the contest and, most importantly, even in selecting the arbitral judge or judges who will hear the case.

In the best-case scenario, highly complex and contentious battles may be resolved in a few months at a fraction of the cost of a trial.

Yet even before the hearings began, it was clear to Gans, who served as chair of the three-person arbitration panel in the case of the communications company and its supplier, that the dispute was a worst-case, not best-case, scenario.

Every motion by one side resulted in two motions by the other. The combatants demanded reams of obscure paper and electronic documents as discovery and added witness after tangential witness to their hearing room lineups.

Before long, collateral disputes erupted, some resulting in court filings. Since both sides bought into this expensive and time-consuming process, the arbitral tribunal could not manage the process efficiently. As the case grew more hopelessly tangled, "We had to stay the arbitration. We told them to fight it out in the courts, and we'll deal with what's left," Gans says.

The case has now developed into a crisis-without-end. After three years, the central question involving defective equipment remains unresolved as of this writing. As with those trench-digging armies of World War I, both companies have paid an extraordinary cost to get nowhere. Aside from the millions of dollars in legal and arbitration fees, and countless hours of staff and management time devoted to collecting documentation, preparing for testimony, and other distractions, the fact is that a business relationship that had been important to both sides has likely been fundamentally and irretrievably impaired.

Gans served as Senior Counsel for Olin Corp. for 12 years and was Vice President, General Counsel, and Secretary for Siemens Corp. from 1979 to 1999. For most of the past decade, he has served as an independent mediator and arbitrator in cases ranging from professional sports contract disputes to battles pitting the nation's largest corporations against each other.

When arbitration spins out of control, he says, the problem often lies with corporate leadership that has not adequately thought out its underlying objectives and/or communicated them to those sectors of the company charged with implementing strategies and policies.

In the communications equipment case, both participants assumed that arbitration, because of its structure and process, would result in a swifter, less costly decision. But they placed too much emphasis on external process and not enough on internal leadership.

"In theory the leaders 'get it.' They know what should be done," Gans says. "They have sophisticated lawyers trained in arbitration and dispute resolution. They have all the right policies in place. But while they talk the talk, they don't walk the walk."

Had the leaders made clear from the outset that their overriding purpose in the dispute was to settle the equipment question with minimum possible distraction and cost, they might have agreed on an arbitration contract that limited discovery to pertinent documents and cut back on legal maneuvers such as extensive deposition and motion practice geared mainly to wear down the opponent.

"In a case involving 10,000 documents, very few of those will actually have a material effect on the case," Gans says. "All of this paper has been generated, all of this staff time spent collecting it, all the lawyers are looking through it and briefing on the issues. At the end of the day, only a very few documents are going to be material to or determine the outcome of the case."

At the start of arbitration, Gans often asks both sides to exchange "reliance documents" – i.e., the ones essential to proving their point. "Then, I ask them to think carefully about what other supplementary documents they need." In the end, though, restraint (and the possibility of a swift resolution) rests with the contestants. Even as Gans spoke to us, he was looking at 10 cartons of documents stacked in his New York office, all from one company that clearly had not gotten the message.

In these situations, leadership is not about playing nice or giving in on matters crucial to your interests. Corporate disputes often involve many millions of dollars and both parties have strong incentives to fight hard and win. But first, they must identify what winning means.

In the past, busy CEOs tended to pass even the most important cases over to inside and outside counsel. Today, most companies realize that the cumulative total of major and minor litigation can have a sizable bottom-line impact. "Nowadays, the general counsel has the ear of both the CEO and the board of directors," says Gans. "And they listen."

A greater problem, Gans believes, is one of attitude, particularly in companies with aggressive, sales-driven cultures. In the absence of focused objectives, win-at-all-costs becomes the rule. Your in-house lawyers will do whatever it takes to win the case at hand, and their hired guns will do the same.

Yet, as Gans points out, civil litigation and arbitration among businesses almost by definition involve people with whom you have important relationships: vendors, suppliers, partners, or customers. Every case that needlessly drags on only makes it harder to salvage the relationship and, possibly, harder to form trusting relationships with others who are now wary of your reputation for combativeness.

By contrast, Gans points to another dispute he handled recently between two Fortune 50 corporations after one purchased a business division from the other. "We adhered to a schedule. It was very adversarial, as it needs to be, but it was done with a view to efficiency and professional respect, one side for the other."

At the outset, the companies themselves limited the time and scope of the case. "They reached agreement on points that should not have to be decided by the arbitrator and which can make the process much more costly," recalls Gans. They stuck to the point in good faith, enabling Gans to quickly get to the heart of the dispute and the issues that truly needed resolving. Although the case was at least as complex as the defective equipment dispute, the entire matter wrapped up in a little over six months.

Even before Gans announced the award, the companies decided to turn the case back to their respective business units to negotiate an amicable compromise, leaving room to salvage the larger business relationship. The very process of respectful exchange during the legal crisis had enabled the sides to find their points of agreement, as well as disagreement, early on, simply because they were willing to focus on business objectives rather than the pure ego rewards of a Pyrrhic victory.

As Gans says, "An enlightened company realizes that these disputes go to the core of its values and integrity, to its competitive standing as a company, and sometimes, even its survival."

—————————— RULE NO. 33 ——————————
LOVE DOES MEAN SAYING YOU'RE SORRY
Owning Up to Error is a Safeguard, Not a Liability

Corporate crises don't come much more serious than the one that beset Odwalla, Inc., in 1996. Dozens of people became violently ill and one Colorado infant died after drinking unpasteurized fruit juice made by the Half Moon Bay, California-based company.

From a business standpoint, the disaster directly undercut Odwalla's core brand identity as a health-friendly, health-conscious manufacturer. In fact, the fatal decision not to pasteurize its products was ostensibly health-related, as the company said pasteurization removed nutrients as well as flavor. Unfortunately, pasteurization would also have likely prevented the contamination, traced back to deadly E. coli bacteria.

The crisis could easily have been Odwalla's undoing, but today the company has returned solidly to its place as a trusted maker of healthy drinks. The resuscitation started with an apology. The company said it was sorry, quickly, clearly, and without qualification. Odwalla did not ponder the legal implications or wait for every stitch of evidence to confirm beyond a shadow of a doubt that they were at fault. In addition to the apology, the company promised to fairly compensate all families affected, and it changed manufacturing processes to prevent future outbreaks. Among the notable steps: flash pasteurization to kill bacteria.

These fundamental recovery actions by no means made Odwalla's problems disappear, nor should they have. The company still faced litigation, costly settlements, and a full share of negative publicity. Slowly, however, the wheel of public perception began to turn from negative back to positive.

"If you look at what people remember [from the case], everyone remembers the positive stuff about what Odwalla did," says Bill Marler, the plaintiff's attorney representing victims and their families in the case.

Marler believes Odwalla's quick and sincere reaction was instrumental in saving the company and the brand. Marler, of the Seattle law firm Marler Clark, ought to know. As the nation's leading plaintiff's attorney in the area of food safety, he has secured nearly $500 million in the past 15 years for clients sickened by tainted products. Having seen many corporate strategies that work well in a litigation crisis, as well as many that backfire, he's too successful to begrudge potential adversaries a few pointed bits of advice, especially if it serves a positive public health purpose.

Many companies mistakenly buy into the myth that a public apology, an offer to pay medical bills, or other expression of regret or responsibility for a mistake will necessarily come back to bite them in court. As a result, they stay mute, hoping to minimize legal damage. Unfortunately, that silence often translates in the court of public opinion as disregard for the well-being of their customers and the public.

Other companies facing litigation crises go on ill-advised offensives. In 2006, for example, Lutheran churchgoers at a social in Minnesota were sickened after eating beef tainted with E. coli. One woman, Carolyn Hawkinson, died. When Marler sued Nebraska Beef Ltd. on behalf of the victims, the company counter-sued, claiming that the church cooks were at fault for improperly handling and preparing the meat. While a Minnesota Department of Health investigation did find the cooks violated some food safety procedures (for example, cutting meatballs open to determine doneness rather than using a thermometer), the department determined that the beef itself was "the most likely source" of the contamination, according to *The New York Times*.

Whatever legal strategy drove the company's decision to sue, there's a fundamental lesson here in public relations: don't blame the hand of God or the hand of a church lady holding a spatula. If a Google search is any indication, by the time Nebraska Beef finally settled with the families of two church members (for an undisclosed sum) in early 2009, journalists, bloggers, and sundry others with opinions to offer had already decided that Nebraska Beef Ltd. was a company that would rather sue pious grandmothers than assume responsibility for its own business.

Marler believes most companies know before the first legal volley has been fired whether they are truly at fault in a given situation. After all, no one has better access to the pertinent facts than the company itself. Those that examine the facts objectively and determine they have done nothing wrong should defend themselves vigorously and uncompromisingly. "Frivolous lawsuits don't help companies, and they don't help society," Marler says. "If you're not at fault, there's no reason to say you're sorry."

If an error on your part has indeed harmed someone, up-front apologies and even promises to make good financially can only help your situation. "When I say this, people sometimes respond, 'Oh, you just want them to admit they're at fault so you can stick it to them.' That's just not the case. If a company is at fault for an injury or death, I get to stick it to them, anyway," Marler says with characteristic bluntness. "You're going to lose. The real question is, by how much?

"In my experience, companies that admit fault, say they're really sorry, and move towards resolution wind up not making the victims quite so angry.... And there's a direct correlation between how [angry] someone is and how much money they want.

"I get so many of my cases because somebody will get poisoned by a company, then reach out to that company and say, 'Will you pay our medical expenses?' And the company says, 'No.' So then they call me up.... The victim may have wanted $10,000 to cover the bills, but now it's a $100,000 or $150,000 case."

Broaden this economic and psychological equation, and

a direct correlation emerges between how angry the public becomes and whether, and how quickly, a company will be able to restore its reputation and protect its brand.

A company that does choose to apologize in a crisis should do so loudly and to everyone who will listen, Marler advises. A terse news release to select old-guard media won't do. Use the social media liberally. "A company should know to have a list of all the people out there who are particularly interested in their products, groups that have websites, Twitter feeds, and Facebook," Marler says. Proactively ask them to suggest ways you can do better. By so doing, you'll not only garner great ideas, you'll also gain advocates for the next time a crisis rolls around.

Most important, make sure that your litigators and the insurance company understand and are fully on board with your approach. Marler cites one case in which a company publicly promised to make good on medical costs incurred by customers due to a faulty product. Unfortunately, the insurance company responded by sending modest checks along with language implying that, by cashing the check, the victims waived any right to further compensation. Not surprisingly, the strategy backfired, as the company was perceived to be totally duplicitous.

The attorneys representing you in court most certainly have your best interests at heart, but they naturally tend to view your interests through a relatively narrow lens of what takes place inside the court room. A legal strategy that makes sense in court could prove to be disastrous to your reputation if you are seen as callous or uncaring. The plaintiffs disappear, but so too do your customers. Only you are guardian of your single most valuable possession: your brand.

That is why you must be the real leader of the litigation team, no matter how tempting it is to hand off the headache to the legal specialists. You must set the tone for how your company navigates the crisis inside and outside the courtroom. "A company with a brand to protect has to look the lawyer in the eye and say, 'This is what I want to see happen,'" advises Marler.

The bottom line is that you don't stop being human just because you're being sued. The threat of litigation has the debilitating effect of causing people and companies to seize up, as if acknowledging so much as a hint of responsibility or concern for a customer who's been wronged will sink your case and expose you to endless liability.

Yet in the end, it's often silence that endangers and obstinacy that destroys a brand.

SECTION EIGHT

UNDER THE GUN
The New Regulatory Climate and Leadership During Public Investigations

"The era of big government is over," President Clinton famously declared in his 1996 State of the Union Address. To paraphrase Mark Twain, that pronouncement was greatly exaggerated.

Of course, government oversight never really went away. But if the best single word to describe the relationship between government and business at the end of the 20th century was "deregulation," the word that fits best one decade later is undoubtedly "compliance".

Complying with myriad government regulations cost U.S. businesses $1.172 trillion in 2008, or roughly eight percent of the U.S. gross domestic product, according to the Competitive Enterprise Institute's 2009 *Ten Thousand Commandments* report. The Federal Register (the compendium of regulations laid down by federal agencies) set a new record of 79,435 pages in 2008, 10 percent higher than in 2007.

The global financial crisis, of course, has only intensified the enthusiasm of politicians and regulators to oversee more and more aspects of private business operations.

We offer these observations not to be polemical in any way but as a simple sign of the times. The era of big government has redoubled, bringing along a host of new global complexities and challenges.

Leaders cannot afford to be passive about compliance in such an environment, says Jim Mintz, founder and president of the James Mintz Group, which helps companies investigate prospective partners and deal with crises. According to Mintz, also a founding member and director of the International Association of Independent Private Sector Inspectors General, "You need to circulate and speak to employees and try to identify specific risks that the company faces. You need to build into the compliance plan ways to address those risks."

A compliance strategy that simply offers generalities about respecting the environment or being honest with the numbers won't do. Strong, specific language is a must, Mintz believes.

Such language must also be backed up with action. "There has to be a culture of compliance that monitors what your people are doing on an ongoing basis, and that welcomes whistle-blowing," Mintz says.

As you'll read in this section, the global nature of today's business raises the stakes exponentially. Ignorance of a foreign law won't protect your company from legal repercussions abroad and at home, if you violate a regulation or even engage a business partner or representative who does so. "The risks are as complex as the opportunities," Mintz says. "One day you need a computer forensics team flying into Arizona and the next day you're looking for an investigative accountant in Azerbaijan."

Mintz is fully aware that some executives don't want to

know how risky business gets done beneath their level and think, for example, that an 800 number welcoming whistle-blower calls is crazy. "Their fear would be that it stirs up a sleeping dog that they want to let lie. They worry they'll stir up irresponsible allegations where people have an axe to grind.

"I would argue that's putting your head in the sand and allowing pressure to build up. All you're doing is creating a bigger and worse crisis down the line. That whistle-blower who has no *internal* number to call may well blow that whistle *externally*, with no notice to the company and far worse consequences." The lesson seems clear: in an age of regulation, wake that compliance dog yourself or it may sneak up and bite you on the…ankle.

RULE No. 34

THE WORLD BELONGS TO THOSE WHO SHOW UP

Don't Fight City Hall and Take an Active Role in Regulation

For corporate executives schooled in free market principles and the virtues of logical decision making, few constituents can be more confounding to deal with than politicians and regulators. They don't own a share of your company, have taken none of the risks involved in building it, and won't be there to accept the blame when some onerous piece of legislation torpedoes your bottom line. Yet, increasingly they seem to demand a voice in every major decision you make.

There's not much point in trying to fight these forces in an age when regulation is intensifying on all fronts, with the strong support of the American people. As Charles Firlotte advises, you'll do your company a lot more good by accepting the reality of government intervention, making friends, and seeking a strong voice in how laws and regulations are handed down. "The world belongs to those who show up," he says. "You need to be part of the action."

Firlotte knows whereof he speaks. As chief executive officer of Aquarion Water Company in Connecticut, he operates one of the most heavily regulated private companies in the United States.

With $180 million in annual revenue and assets in excess of $1 billion, Aquarion supplies drinking water to residents of three states in the Northeast. The company performs some 150,000 government-mandated tests of the water supply each year and checks for more than 100 possible contaminants mandated for testing by local, state, and federal governments. That, by the way, is a 500 percent increase over the 20 or so contaminants they checked for just two decades ago.

In addition to the health and safety issues, Aquarion, as a utility, is also closely regulated on the financial front. In other words, every important step the company takes has political or regulatory overtones.

While Firlotte understands the inevitable, and even beneficial, role that regulation plays in the water system ("It's the only utility product that people actually ingest"), prospering in such an environment requires an almost preternatural sensitivity to the needs and agendas of bureaucrats and politicians.

Most of the regulators he deals with sincerely believe in their underlying mission to ensure public safety. At the same time, they operate under enormous pressure not to approve new procedures or policy changes that could backfire. They are extremely cautious as a result. "They're highly sensitive to public perception and criticism. And they live in a fairly nasty political world where politicians will take shots at them," says Firlotte.

Politicians, of course, have their own agendas. "You really have to be alert as to who the legislators are who has an interest in your industry," Firlotte says. "You have to know who the guys are that count. For me it's who's on the environmental committee? Who's on the health committee?"

Firlotte and Aquarion walked that fine line a couple of years ago when pushing for a regulatory change. Instead of seeking a rate increase every time the company needed to replace pipes or other infrastructure, Aquarion wanted the ability to add small surcharges directly to customers' bills.

The plan made perfect sense from a business and consumer perspective. Formally raising rates is a "long, bureaucratic, and very costly process" involving multiple aspects of state government. The surcharge would add flexibility, reduce costs, and encourage companies to replace aging infrastructure. A classic win-win. Yet there were political risks.

First, Firlotte approached the financial regulators and pointed out that a half dozen other states had implemented similar changes. The regulators said the plan was good, but they wanted to know that legislators were on board.

Next, Firlotte spoke with some key legislators in Hartford. They, too, liked the idea. Not surprisingly, they too wanted cover. What the politicians obviously feared most was a backlash from angry customers. Firlotte stressed that the surcharges would be small and that newer pipes and other equipment would minimize leaks, thereby improving water safety and the environment at the same time. Moreover, the small surcharges would mean fewer trips to Hartford for rate increases, which inevitably draw close scrutiny from the media.

By delicately pushing the agenda with both regulators and politicians, the company was able to encourage legislation that passed in 2008.

Firlotte knows as well as anyone how challenging the government can be as a business partner. "Every year you get legislation and you wonder how it ever got airborne. Wacky stuff that could do significant harm to your business," Firlotte says. Having a voice requires patience and care. "If you're sensitive to the needs of the legislator, you have that discourse with the regulator, and you're among those who show up, part of that world can belong to you."

RULE No. 35
WHEN FACTS DON'T MATTER, FORGET THE FACTS
In Government Relations, Pragmatism is King

In the previous chapter, we discussed how artful diplomacy and understanding can help push your agenda and protect your interests amid the maze of government interests. Unfortunately, there are times when common sense is commonly useless. All the facts may be on your side but, in the political world, pragmatism rules. Your natural inclination may be to dig your heels in and fight. But a moral victory won't mean much if it engulfs you in a debilitating and costly struggle.

That was the lesson learned by one company, a recognized leader in the business of rating how well companies in a specific industry group (we've masked the details) perform. Not long ago, this ratings company undertook a massive overhaul of its system in order to provide more scientific, accurate, and reliable results. In other words, they strove for excellence. Justly proud, the company expected the revamped system to be uniformly greeted as a landmark advance in the science of rating performance.

No sooner was the new system unveiled than howls of protest

erupted from some minority-owned companies because their performance ratings had suddenly dropped. The new system must be racially biased, they claimed. The charges shocked the ratings company. After all, the whole point of the revisions, the months and months of hard work and effort and expense, had been to make the ratings *less* subjective, less prone to racial or any other type of bias. The ratings company stood firm, offering to show any and all interested parties exactly how it had arrived at the new system.

The numbers obviously revealed some inherent weaknesses in the offended companies' operations, they suggested. But the offended companies had no interest in such hows, whens, and whys. Politically well-connected, they began making phone calls. In no time at all, the ratings firm heard from the state attorney general.

Once again, the company explained its metrics. Look at our research! Look at our numbers! Look at our results! Unfortunately, the AG was no more interested in the science behind the ratings than were the companies that were complaining. "Just let me know what you're going to do about this," he said. The AG wanted positive publicity for himself, but he also wanted the problem resolved before it became a sensitive political event.

A crisis management consultant convinced the ratings firm to play ball. The firm would offer to work directly with the minority companies on strategies to bring up their numbers while providing the attorney general with nine steps to help do so. The firm would also make a donation to a nonprofit organization providing educational opportunities for disadvantaged students interested in joining the industry.

Perhaps all this conciliatory action seemed unfair to the managers of the ratings company. But they were pragmatic withal, enough so to smooth out ruffled feathers and keep a dustup from developing into a real crisis. Politicians are the ultimate pragmatists. Choose your battles carefully.

RULE NO. 36

IT'S A SMALLER WORLD, AFTER ALL

The FCPA is a Defining Test of Global Leadership Amid Global Crises

---

The U.S. government's high-profile criminal case against American entrepreneur Frederic Bourke in 2009 had all the makings of classic film noir, replete with Midas-like wealth, foreign oil contracts, Chechen mobsters, and suitcases full of cash for payoffs to officials in remote Azerbaijan.

Yet, business owners and executives who followed the case might have found the most chilling aspect in the few simple words attributed by *Bloomberg* to a juror who helped convict Bourke of conspiring to bribe foreign leaders in an Azerbaijan oil deal during the late 1990s: "We thought he knew and definitely *could have known. He's an investor. It's his job to know* [emphasis ours]."

The same law that snared Bourke – the U.S. Foreign Corrupt Practices Act (FCPA) – presents a nonstop crisis-in-waiting for any company operating overseas. There's little or no cover for U.S. corporations and executives who allow corrupt practices to take place in their name, even if the executives themselves have no specific knowledge of these practices, and even if those practices take place in some obscure republic where a fistful of under-the-table dollars is as much a part of business as a morning coffee.

In fact, no law more vividly defines the communications challenges that face and define business leadership in today's world. To truly be a leader on this high-stakes front, you must commandeer comprehensive interdiction and compliance programs and, if those programs are to be effective, you must make it patently clear to every relevant party – including the regulators who may someday target the company, as well as your internal constituents – that you are deadly serious about compliance.

"If management says, 'We've got to be ethical, wink, wink, nod, nod,' people will understand that they can cut corners as long as they don't get caught," says Lucinda Low, a partner in the Washington office of Steptoe & Johnson LLP, and one of the nation's leading authorities on the FCPA and other international anti-corruption laws. "If management says, 'We're going to compete vigorously but comply with the law,' that's totally different."

"The consequences can be very, very significant, including criminal penalties for the company and for management," adds Low. "They may lose their jobs. There may be loss of eligibility to participate in government programs or World Bank contracts, or loss of ability to export. Those are some of the kinds of consequences that can fall on companies and management if they don't comply."

Any company engaged in overseas business of any kind must therefore have a vigorous international compliance program backed up at the highest levels of management and communicated to every employee.

Companies design these programs in different ways. Some assign a committee; others appoint an individual to monitor international compliance. The program may or may not be administered through your general counsel. Most important, however, everyone who represents your company as an employee, as well as all your outside contractors, must know exactly what to do and who to call any time they encounter an ethical gray zone. You are only inviting disaster when representatives in remote areas make difficult decisions on your behalf, without counsel. "I call that 'horseback lawyering,'" Low says. "This could be putting the company at risk."

The FCPA, designed to prevent businesses with U.S. operations from engaging in corruption overseas, was first enacted in the late 1970s and expanded a decade later. In many ways, Low says, the act is just now coming of age in an ever-more-integrated global marketplace. "New international cooperation makes it easier to discover, investigate, and prosecute these activities effectively."

The FCPA "is being applied very broadly and enforced in a very vigorous way," adds Low, whose firm represented an ancillary party in the Bourke case. For example, prosecutors never suggested that Bourke, a Greenwich, Connecticut millionaire perhaps best known as co-founder of handbag maker Dooney & Bourke, actually hauled the money-stuffed suitcases to Azerbaijan or even formally approved any bribes. Yet the leadership burden was all about the possibility that, as the juror noted, he *could* have known. Understood in those terms, there can be no heavier leadership burden or crisis management responsibility.

The scope and reach of current foreign anti-corruption laws also make companies and their leaders responsible, not just for the actions of their own employees, but for subsidiaries and contractors hired to represent the company. "You really have to ask yourself, 'What are my employees and my third parties... doing in the most remote corners of the world in which we operate?'" Low says.

Your "knowledge" of potentially corrupt practices takes on a special and ominous legal meaning. "The technical legal standard is willful ignorance," says Low. "What that means is you can't put your head in the sand. It can't be 'hear no evil, see no evil, speak no evil.' You have to take active steps to prevent third parties from doing these things."

Sometimes, bribery seems to be widespread and systemic within a corporation. In late 2008, the German engineering giant Siemens was hit with an unprecedented $800 million in fines under the FCPA for bribing foreign officials in no fewer than 10 countries, involving sales of everything from medical devices in Russia to metro trains in China. In the wake of the scandal, Siemens vowed sweeping changes in its practices.

In other instances, by contrast, companies may face stiff fines and, more important, damage to their reputations for the actions of relatively obscure subsidiaries doing deals that don't merit more than a footnote on the overall balance sheet.

In 2005, Monsanto, the St. Louis-based agricultural giant, agreed to a $1.5 million fine after one of its managers and an independent promotional company in Indonesia hired by Monsanto bribed a Jakarta official in hopes of easing the way for sales of genetically modified cotton. The fact that Monsanto, to its credit, learned of the incident and reported it to U.S. authorities didn't prevent the case from becoming a highly public embarrassment that reverberated all the way to its corner offices in St. Louis.

Similarly, Westinghouse Air Brake Technologies Corp. was hit with a $300,000 fine in 2008 after a Calcutta subsidiary bribed members of the India Railway Board in hopes of fatter contracts and fewer tax audits.

Legally speaking, it's no excuse that your company is large or that you, as CEO, have a thousand other responsibilities on your plate. Nor can a company or its leaders expect legal cover from the simple fact that bribery and corruption are standard practice in many countries and regions.

"The world is a difficult place. In some parts, this kind of corruption problem is demand-driven. You have regulatory systems that are opaque, government officials who aren't paid a living wage and are expected to try to supplement their incomes," Low says. "Sometimes there are real physical threats, as well as economic consequences" for those who refuse to play along.

Regardless, international companies are bound to rise above local customs or else face the prospect of stiff sanctions back home. Officials at American Rice, based in Texas, may have thought they were only following the crowd when it was selling rice to Haiti, where corruption, poverty, and political strife are perennial facts of life. "There was a view that most companies bringing rice in were smuggling it in, not declaring it, or undervaluing it," Low says. "And that's what this company did."

In the end, two senior executives were convicted in federal court on criminal charges of bribing Haitian officials into looking the other way. "The fact that everybody was doing it wasn't a defense," says Low, who represented one of the executives. "It cost the company, and it cost the senior executives."

We've focused on the FCPA because it is the oldest and most sweeping international anti-corruption law. Increasingly, though, additional laws in the United States, as well as measures enacted by other countries, are adding to a crowded field of rules and regulations governing ethics in international business dealings.

While there are no guarantees against international legal issues arising, "the fact that you have an effective compliance program mitigates penalties substantially," Low says. "You can translate that into dollar-for-dollar benefits."

You should sleep a little sounder at night knowing you've minimized the risk of one day hearing a prosecutor, judge, or juror utter the words, *You could have known. You're the CEO. It's your job to know.*

SECTION NINE

INTERNAL LEADERSHIP

Of all the leadership and communications challenges that executives face, none are more delicate and personal than those involving your own staff. The liabilities are significant, but so are the opportunities to positively affect the future of your company – not just through formal pronouncements and written communications but through the decisive messages that your everyday manner and disposition send so strongly.

Christine Lewis-Varley, a management consultant who has worked with executives and employees around the world, recalls how one executive of a large company created, perhaps unknowingly, a loyal lifelong employee for the price of a soda.

The executive had bought pizza for his staff after asking them to stay late one night to work on an important project. Along with the pizzas, the executive provided several large bottles of Coca-Cola and one can of Pepsi, which he placed on the desk of one of the workers.

"I noticed that you don't drink Coke," he said. "I brought you a Pepsi instead."

Years later, the beneficiary of that soft drink was still showing emotion when he related the story to Lewis-Varley. "I thought, if this man is that concerned about me, and about details, I am going to follow him," the employee said. "I want to be on his team. I've worked for him for 15 years."

Such influence carries with it a corresponding burden. Executives unaware of how closely they're being scrutinized, or simply oblivious to their employees, can unintentionally dry up the channels of communication and de-motivate their people to actively support and implement their goals.

Lewis-Varley, who recently was appointed Director of Human Resource for the Governor's Office of Homeland Security and Emergency Preparedness in Louisiana, recalls another executive who asked for her help in motivating the employees of his consulting firm.

After five minute in a staff meeting, Lewis-Varley spotted the problem. Simply enough, none of the employees understood what the President was saying. A brilliant scientist, he had built a successful business helping major corporations take full advantage of the intellectual property generated by their research departments.

"He had a very clear picture in his own mind of what he did and where he was going. But he didn't have the capacity to understand that the people who worked with him didn't see with the same set of eyes or hear with the same set of ears," Lewis-Varley says.

"They didn't really even know what their jobs were," says Lewis-Varley.

"I have found that so many times inside organizations," she adds. Don't expect employees to volunteer if they are confused, particularly in the worst job market of our collective lives. "People don't want to leave or risk their jobs. Very often they'll go along with things that they really don't understand."

The President addressed the problem by consciously getting to know his employees as individuals. By taking the time to speak with them rather than pontificate, and by learning their preferences (Coke or Pepsi, so to speak), he learned how each one of them learned best, and he learned to intuit when they were confused or needed more elaboration. Over time, he turned his staff from a group of paycheck collectors into a motivated workforce ready to carry his vision forward.

Think about that cookie incident, related in the opening pages of this book. Yes, cookies matter. So do soft drinks.

RULE No. 37

CONSENSUS AND INFLUENCE ARE MORE POWERFUL THAN AUTHORITY

They'll Comply With Orders, But They'll Win With Goals

Ed Kangas learned one of his most valuable leadership lessons by watching a group of six-year-olds chase a soccer ball around a field.

The boys darted around the ball in a shapeless, formless scrum, a furious mass of energy going nowhere. Then a father removed a soccer goal from the trunk of his car. Without saying a word, he placed the goal at the far end of the field.

"Suddenly one little boy said, 'Look!' They all pointed," recalls Kangas, whose own son was on the field that day. "The next thing you know, that herd of boys was moving right down the field toward the goal."

For Kangas, this simple anecdote dramatizes a vital distinction that leaders need bear in mind: the difference between authority and the power of consensus. A coach with a whistle around his neck might have had the *authority* to tell the boys what to do and where on the field to go, but the placement of a goal generated the *consensus* to get them all moving together as though it was their idea. "When a group of people agree upon a goal, there's almost nothing that will stop them," he says.

Over the years, Kangas has had innumerable opportunities as a corporate leader and board member to put this idea into practice. A highly sought-after corporate director, Kangas today serves as chairman of the board of directors of Tenet Healthcare, one of the nation's largest private hospital companies, as well on the board of United Technologies, Intuit, and several other companies. Never was the concept of goal-oriented leadership more important to Kangas than during the 1990s when, as CEO of the global accounting enterprise Deloitte Touche Tohmatsu, he was faced with transforming the firm. Deloitte needed to become a truly global firm instead of a collection of accounting practices.

Because accounting laws vary widely from country to country, the individual country practices of an international firm traditionally operate with significant independence. When dealing with the audits of a major international client, each Deloitte office would supply its own audit of operations in the separate countries.

"You might have 25 separate audits coming in from around the world," Kangas says. That system worked fine until major client companies began integrating their overseas operations, placing less emphasis on national borders and more on flexibility and the ability to respond quickly to global markets.

"As our clients globalized and started operating in global computer, accounting, purchasing, and manufacturing platforms, they were expecting their auditors to behave as a global organization as well," says Kangas. Global business demanded truly global accounting firms. To Kangas and other top leaders, the challenge was clear: operate globally across borders or lose major clients.

Despite the clarity of that challenge, the company faced a delicate and difficult internal process of convincing proud, traditional partners around the world to give up autonomy in the interests of greater effectiveness for the entire firm.

The most direct and obvious move might have been a straightforward mandate. After all, the United States was the company's largest practice and generated 40 percent of its revenues. Just as surely, though, Kangas believed that dictating the answer could never generate the sort of team effort required to reinvent the firm. Such a move might even destroy it. Back then, "Partners were very protective of their national rights. You couldn't tell them what to do," Kangas says.

Instead, Kangas embarked on a long, slow process over the next several years that involved almost constant travel (120 visits to Japan alone, by his estimate) to every Deloitte practice, visiting overseas offices on their own territory, to understand their concerns and, just as important, to communicate his own belief in their importance to the company.

"Authority may flow from the top down, but real power flows from the bottom up," says Kangas. "Leaders are empowered by the people they lead. A CEO gets his authority from the board of directors, but his power will be based on his ability to influence those in his company based on his competence, the trust they place in him, and on respect. If a CEO uses this power to influence, he'll be much more effective than using authority."

Instead of having the audits of the branches of individual clients controlled by the various offices in every country, Kangas championed a model in which the partner leading each major international client would take the global lead in managing that client. So if a client was based in France, a partner in Deloitte's Paris office would have the authority to lead Deloitte teams in New York, Tokyo, or anywhere else doing work for the same client.

This move effectively neutralized objections that the global strategy was simply a U.S. power grab. Further, the American operation, though representing 40 percent of Deloitte's revenue, voluntarily reduced its voting power on the board of directors to 20 percent. A global management team, made up of partners from many countries, was developed.

As Deloitte's representatives began to trust the motives and vision of Kangas and his colleagues in the leadership, they began to buy into the mission without being told to do so. This trust allowed the global leadership to gain important objectives. For example, world leaders agreed to empower the global CEO to remove country CEOs – a crucial step if Deloitte was to become a truly global company.

The process of transforming Deloitte lasted through most of the 1990s but ultimately paid off as the company positioned itself to meet the needs of 21st century clients. "As CEO, I found that taking time to build consensus around the goal was very important. It may have taken longer to make decisions that way, but it shortened implementation time dramatically," says Kangas, who is now retired from Deloitte and serves on a number of corporate boards.

"If you give me the choice of influence or authority, I'll take influence any time. If you have the authority, they will *probably* do what you tell them to do. If you have great influence, based on respect, trust, competence and loyalty, you can build the emotional and intellectual consensus to do almost anything."

————————— Rule No. 38 —————————
The Higher You Go, the Blinder You Get

Attributes That Make for Personal Success Often Backfire During Crises

The founder and CEO of a large, successful company could not understand why communications within the organization seemed so stilted. When Marshall Goldsmith, a consultant to managers at some of the world's largest companies, traced the problem back to the CEO himself, the man was incredulous.

"What do they mean I 'squelch communication!'" he snapped. "I was captain of the debate team at Cambridge! Nobody loves a good debate more than I do!"

Of course, he was making Goldsmith's point. "He was a CEO and entrepreneur worth hundreds of millions of dollars," Goldsmith says. "Imagine that I'm three levels below you. I express an opinion, and you go into debate mode. What chance do I have? In your mind, this may be a debate. In my mind I'm just getting stepped on."

That's just one example of what Goldsmith, author of *What Got You Here Won't Get You There*, refers to as CEO blind spots, areas that, left unattended, erode rather than enhance leadership. Ironically, these blind spots are often directly related to the hard-charging, competitive qualities that helped a person rise in the first place.

Leadership, once attained, requires a subtler touch, Goldsmith explains. The process starts with identifying some of the essential blind spots, including:

Winning too much. You don't get to be CEO of a company of any size (or C-suite resident or director, for that matter) unless you are a winner. "CEOs are great competitors, and their desire to compete and win has helped them become successful," Goldsmith says. "They want to win if the situation is meaningful, critical, or even if it's not important. They just want to win." While that drive continues to be an asset in battling external competitors for market share, it can become a serious liability within your own ranks, especially in a crisis, Goldsmith advises.

"During a crisis, people tend to react more emotionally. When we become emotional under stress, we're more likely to kick back into what worked in the past. In other words, we're more likely to be in the mode of, 'I'm going to win, I'm going to carry this ball.'" Yet this is the very time when you need your staff to be winners, and that can't happen unless you hand *them* the ball.

Because you are the leader, and the boss, you will prevail during just about any internal conflict or battle that's important enough to you. Yet that guarantee, with the tacit self-confidence it reinforces, should liberate you from the *need* to win. When necessary, defer, and hold back your power for another day. "It's very important to let go of this incredible drive toward achievement," Goldsmith says. "You don't have to be the champion all the time."

Adding too much value. Chief executives naturally feel compelled to add value to any conversation. "Instead of saying, 'That's a great idea,' your natural tendency is to say, 'That's a nice idea, why don't you add this to it,'" Goldsmith says.

You may intend your words as a suggestion to be used if helpful or else discarded. Unfortunately, in the real world, there is no such thing as a CEO's "suggestion."

As the retired CEO of a major pharmaceutical company lamented to Goldsmith, "My suggestions all become orders, even if I didn't want them to be." Every comment you make regarding an idea or an initiative imposes an implicitly automatic burden on the person implementing the project to rethink and re-plan based on your input. "Effectiveness of execution is a function of A, the quality of the idea, times B, the commitment required to make it work," Goldsmith says. "If we get too wrapped up in improving the quality of the idea by just a little, we may damage the commitment by a whole lot."

Of course, there are times when your suggestions are vital. You cannot be endorsing half-baked ideas just to spare people's feelings. But the key, Goldsmith says, is not to "add value" reflexively. "Stop and breathe. Look in the other person's eyes and ask yourself, 'What is my comment going to do to their commitment?' If your comment is going to decrease their commitment, ask, 'Is it worth it?' Sometimes it is worth it. If you stop and think for a few seconds you generally get the right answer."

Starting with *no, but,* and *however.* Goldsmith tried an experiment during one session with a CEO client. The man would be fined $20 each time he started a sentence with "no," "but," or "however."

The idea was to show how unthinkingly we use these terms and, by extension, how unintentionally damaging they can be. "When someone speaks to us and the first word out of his or her mouth is, 'No,' what does that mean to us? *You're wrong.* What does 'but' mean? *Disregard everything you just said.* 'However' is just a fancy word for 'but,'" says Goldsmith.

While these oppositional words can be slightly irritating when exchanged among professional equals, they destroy communication in the inherently unequal exchange between CEO and employee, Goldsmith says.

It may seem unfair to be judged by what you see as merely verbal tics, but the game of leadership is won or lost as easily in nuance and gesture as in the sweep of major decisions – and that includes the unspoken "no," the unspoken "but," and the unspoken "however" that register consciously or not in your gestures and your facial expressions.

"A lot of being a CEO is boring," observes Goldsmith. "You're sitting in a room watching PowerPoint presentations for hour after hour on subjects you already know about. You're thinking, *I want to go to the bathroom.* The reality is that, even though you're bored, everybody's looking at your face. If you look bored or uninterested or checked-out, they'll all be demoralized."

Making sure your face expresses engagement and interest isn't about being phony. It's about understanding in a very professional way that your role is vitally symbolic. Your attention to small verbal and facial clues becomes even more important during a crisis, Goldsmith adds. "Your direct reports are afraid for their jobs. So you have to be very, very sensitive that you don't take already heightened fear and make it worse."

How did the CEO fare in his *no, but, however* challenge? At the end of 90 minutes, he owed Goldsmith $420 for 21 infractions.

Playing favorites. When Alan Mulally first moved from Boeing to Ford in 2006, he asked his managers to color reports in green (for success), orange (for caution), or red (for projects in trouble).

After the first couple of meetings produced a sea of green reports, Mulally asked the managers why a company with nothing but successful projects was hemorrhaging billions of dollars. Here was a leader who preferred painful truths to comforting fairy tales.

"Every company and every leader says they hate suck-ups," Goldsmith says. "So, why are there so many suck-ups? It's because we tend to reinforce people who reinforce us. We see this quality in other people, but we have a hard time seeing it in ourselves."

It's an especially insidious blind spot, because it results in the corollary tendency among CEOs to play favorites. "As you rise in a corporation, this trap only gets bigger," Goldsmith says. Without even trying, you may find yourself surrounded by people who subtly, and in a thousand small ways, insulate you from bad news, until it's too late. Goldsmith adds, "In a crisis, you really need to hear the truth."

By praising those with the nerve to hand you the red reports, you take a large step toward protecting yourself from those who would over-protect you.

Clinging to the past. The fully justified sense of accomplishment that comes with reaching a leadership position can create its own hazard that Goldsmith calls "the superstition trap." It is the persistent belief that, because one has succeeded, all or most of the traits or behaviors one has adopted in the past contributed to that success. A successful leader who is courageous, brilliant, and deaf in one ear might fall into the trap by concluding that being deaf in one year is an indispensable ingredient in the recipe for success – and start demanding it from others.

"Any human or animal will replicate behaviors that are followed by constant reinforcement. The more successful we are, and the more positive reinforcement we get, the more we fall into this trap," Goldsmith says.

The superstition trap, if indulged, can stunt personal growth and professional development. If you are a fully developed leader on the first day you're in office, why bother to get better? In a broader sense, a reluctance to examine and correct personal flaws ripples through the entire company. They see your complacency and they model it. Remember that everyone around you is paying attention to your every act and utterance. If you want them to get better, set the example, Goldsmith suggests.

"The best leaders I work with are always asking, *how can I get better?*" he says.

Consider Kent Kresa, who took over the leadership of Northrup Grumman in 1990 when the lumbering defense giant appeared headed for oblivion. "Rather than talking about how smart he was, he talked about what he could do better, his own areas of improvement. He asked people to help him rather than telling people what to do and how to do it." By so doing, he created a powerful model for self-improvement that helped Kresa and his team return Northrup Grumman to profitability. In fact, he transformed the corporate culture altogether.

Confidential, anonymous feedback can be extremely helpful in highlighting areas you could work on, Goldsmith adds. "Instead of leadership by preaching, try leadership by living."

Rule No. 39

Kissing Up and Kicking Down Are Not Allowed

Servant Leadership

By the time a crisis occurs, it's too late to ask your employees and customers to start believing in your mission. They either do or they don't – and whether they do or don't may well determine your chances for survival. Companies are thus well-advised to use their peacetime wisely to fortify the confidence and commitment of all vital stakeholders.

"Servant leadership," espoused by executives such as James H. Blanchard, former chairman and CEO of Synovus, a major bank holding company based in Georgia, is a holistic strategy for doing just that. Some 15 years before the current financial crisis erupted, Blanchard sent a clear warning to every supervisor in the company: treat your workers with respect and dignity or you are gone.

Regardless of whether a manager was generating the best numbers in the company or barely scraping by, Synovus would no longer tolerate their saying all the right things to superiors only to return to their own departments and berate or abuse the staff.

"We call that saluting the flag and kicking the dog," Blanchard says. "We decided that people who were inclined to supervise like that just didn't have a place in our company."

Blanchard put his own credibility and reputation on the line by making this announcement, not behind closed doors at an executive retreat, but before the entire company. "I remember standing up and saying, 'if we don't fulfill that commitment to you as team members, you have no reason to believe anything I ever tell you.'"

Thus began the company's formal experiment with servant leadership, a concept developed more than 40 years ago by philosopher Robert K. Greenleaf, who stressed that positions of authority carry obligations rather than entitlements.

Servant leadership defines the supervisory mission in terms of helping subordinates succeed and achieve through appreciation and reinforcement, not intimidation. Instead of focusing exclusively on correcting weaknesses (a losing proposition, in Blanchard's view), leadership training courses encourage supervisors to recognize and build on the strengths of their people.

At the CEO level, servant leadership is defined by the "attitude that 'I am here at the pleasure of the board, I am here to respond to my constituents and benefit shareholders, customers, and employees,'" Blanchard says. "'I'm a custodian.'"

In the months following Blanchard's announcement, many supervisors, including some highly intelligent and successful performers, balked at the new regime. Some left Synovus voluntarily; others were shown the door. The core of employees and supervisors who remained is committed to principles that have become a guiding force at Synovus.

Synovus is not a self-realization workshop. It is a multibillion dollar business. It has serious fiscal responsibilities and it meets those responsibilities. "We demand a lot, and we expect a lot from our employees, and we require excellence," Blanchard says. "What we're really saying is the old command and control type of supervision is not wanted here."

As it turns out, what's good for people is good for business. In 2008, Synovus was ranked number 15 on *U.S. Banker Magazine*'s "Top 100 Banks." A year earlier, Synovus ranked in the top 20 of *ABA Banking Journal*'s "Top Performers" and earned a spot on Fortune's annual "Best Companies to Work for in America." Blanchard, who retired in 2006 as chairman but remains on the board, has received a number of prominent leadership awards.

"If you're doing servant leadership as just another management style to get more out of folks, it won't wash," he says. "But if you're doing it because you think it's the right thing to do, it's a win-win. People give more of themselves for the good of the organization. Your productivity increases, and your customer satisfaction increases."

Nobody, least of all James Blanchard, believes that servant leadership or any other management philosophy by itself could have prevented the current economic crisis. But it's the companies focused on short-term returns versus long-term principles and goals that pay the highest penalty when the economy goes bad.

In an age where public opinion can be made or broken by a single event or statement going viral in the social media, arrogant, self-entitled managers put the very principles of capitalism and freedom on trial. Blanchard, for one, believes the tenets of servant leadership may be our best hope to right that course.

Many other leaders who have never heard the term "servant leadership" have already incorporated its philosophy in dealing with employees and customers, and averted possible crises along the way. To be sure, the implications of servant leadership extend well beyond internal management and speak to the ethics with which companies treat their markets.

For example, when Toro a few years back learned that some older model ride-on lawnmowers might be subject to rolling over, then-CEO Ken Melrose directed the company to install expensive rollover protection systems free to anyone who owned one of those models, regardless of how long they'd owned it or from whom they bought it.

"Wall Street was unhappy," Melrose told MBA students in a 2006 speech at Bethel University. But "we were doing the right, right thing." While the motive was humanitarian, it's not hard to understand that the cost of those systems is minimal in comparison with the potential damage that could be caused when a consumer is tragically injured and a company appears not to care.

Melrose also began using servant leadership as Blanchard did: internally, to remake the corporate culture. He began to act, and act dynamically, from the moment he took over Toro as an ailing (many said dying) company in the early 1980s. His first cost-cutting acts were to eliminate management perks such as company jets and big bonuses. Such actions sent a clear message: I am here to serve the company. So armed, Melrose was also better able to make the necessary job and budget cuts to return Toro to profitability, without alienating rank and file employees.

It's debatable to what extent the majority of current corporate leaders in the U.S. reflects the views and strategies of a James Blanchard and a Ken Melrose, or how many of them are just less flamboyant versions of Bernie Ebbers – less flamboyant, but comparably appetitive, self-interested, and dangerous. The fraud Ebbers perpetrated led to a spectacular corporate collapse in 2002 that ultimately cost WorldCom and its shareholders billions, and resulted in what was then the largest bankruptcy in American history (along with a 25-year jail sentence for Ebbers).

"Every time we go through a crisis that involves fraud or malfeasance, it not only damages the people and the companies involved, but the entire system that has made us the greatest, most affluent nation on the face of the earth," Blanchard says. "Everything is fragile. When fire touches wood, it burns. When corruption and deceit touch the free enterprise system, it takes a chink out of the armor. And that's where we are today."

"I think very few executives, as a percentage of the total, have abused the privileges of the offices that they've held," adds Blanchard. "The very few but very prominent [exceptions] have smudged everyone. The truth is that CEOs have been so demonized that it will take years to recover."

Whether you call it servant leadership or just good business practice, a population of CEOs with more servants and fewer commanders may be our best hope, Blanchard believes. "That kind of sensibility can restore reputations that have been damaged so badly in the last few years. I think that's good for the country. I know it's good for the free enterprise system."

——————— RULE NO. 40 ———————

PEOPLE WANT TO BE INSPIRED
Your Soldiers Must Help Choose the Mission

Jody Davids rose to one of the top leadership posts at the medical giant Cardinal Health in Ohio, overseeing a team of some 2,000 workers as Executive Vice President and CIO. But her most important lesson on leadership came from someone with no business experience at all – her son.

Lance Corporal Wesley G. Davids joined the Marine Corps right out of high school in 2003. "He was extremely angry after September 11, 2001, and he wanted to do something about it," Davids recalls.

A champion rower and excellent student, Wesley scored well enough on a military entrance exam to be offered college scholarships, flight school, and officer training. He chose the infantry instead. "He wanted to go after bad guys. In the Marine Corps, the infantry is the most revered position. He wanted to be part of that."

Just 10 weeks after deploying to Iraq with Ohio's Lima Company in March 2005, Wesley died when his transport vehicle, patrolling the treacherous Al Anbar Province, ran over a buried bomb. "He was killed the day after he turned 20," Davids says. "There were 12 or 13 guys riding in the vehicle. Six were killed, and the rest were severely injured and sent home."

In July, as the grieving family struggled with the loss, a box of Wesley's personal effects arrived from Iraq. Along with his uniform, boots, Bible, CDs, and other items, was a letter from Wesley, addressed to them.

"If you are reading this letter, then the worst has happened," it began.

Davids says, "In the letter he goes on to describe how proud he is of what he's doing, how he's finally found the key to happiness. He says we should not be angry about his death, because nobody made him do it. He fully understood the risks when he went into the service. He wrote how great he felt about himself."

She adds, "It was a wonderful letter to receive. I would say that it has changed my life in a lot of ways. First, as a mom, I know he wasn't hating it there or regretting having made the decision. He was in a good frame of mind. He was doing something he loved to do and that he felt was meaningful."

Later, she began to see inspirational meaning in Wesley's experience – not in his death but in his life. "I came back to my role in corporate America as the leader of a very large group. I thought, what do I learn from this? I have a son who went to the absolute worst conditions I could imagine. It was 110 degrees and he was living in terrible situations. When they're out there on the front lines, it's not barracks; it's not comfortable at all. He was eating MREs [Meals Ready to Eat]. He was working very hard, and there was danger every place he turned. He knew he could die at any instant. Why was he so happy and even inspired to be doing what he was doing?"

Then she thought of her own staff. "I have every incentive [to offer them] that I can imagine: pay, comfort, soft chairs, Internet access, coffee shops in the building, whatever people want. And sometimes my people aren't as motivated as my son was in that very tough situation."

The more she thought about it, the more Davids began to realize that the essence of leadership is the ability to inspire people to make sacrifices, not for fear of losing their jobs or because they are given an order, nor even in expectation of a promotion or a raise, but because they feel so in tune with your goals that they would not have it any other way.

"I'm asking people to do extraordinary things. I'm asking them to meet project deadlines that are just seemingly impossible, or do it on a low budget, or spend the weekend fixing something that broke. I'm asking them to work over the weekend, or over the Christmas holidays, to miss their kids' birthday parties or soccer games. Those are all sacrifices," she says. "I had always believed my job was to get people to achieve the mission at hand.

"The new part of my thinking is that what's really important is to get them to *choose* the mission."

Davids says that anyone in a leadership position starts with an inherent advantage: "People *want* to be inspired. They want to feel that they are part of something bigger than themselves."

The first task, she adds, is to make sure that everyone in your organization has a clear understanding, not just of their own tasks, but of the overall vision and values of your organization. That means developing and communicating your vision so clearly and strongly that everyone who comes on board takes part ownership of the mission. "That is why my son joined the Marine Corps. Their culture constantly reinforces the history and the traditions, all of the ideals that the Marines represent."

A fundamental belief in the opportunity for team victory is another critical component. "People want to know they can win. Nobody wants to be involved in a hopeless battle, and that's another lesson I learned from my son's experience. They sincerely believe that if anybody can win, it's them." They do not need to believe that victory is assured, but they do need to be guided by a clear and persuasive idea, and that victory for the team is reasonably attainable.

Davids also came to believe less in the overriding importance of hierarchies and titles. Though organizational structure, whether in a military unit or a corporation, is crucial, during a time of great challenge those distinctions became far less important than the capabilities, strengths, and weaknesses of the people behind the titles.

"I became so much more connected to my team," she says. "I know them more as people. They have the ability to inspire me, because my eyes are open. And my heart is open, in a way that it wasn't before."

Wesley's example was so powerful and, despite the tragedy of his death, so positive, that Davids' younger son, Steven, has since become a Marine. As of this writing, Davids was preparing to leave her post at Cardinal Health in order to devote herself full-time to studying and talking about leadership – a journey inspired by her son.

AFTERWORD
In a New World, Old Values Are More Vital Than Ever

Shortly after taking over as presiding judge for the 304th District Juvenile Court in Dallas County, Texas in 2006, William A. Mazur looked at a youthful offender standing before him and asked, "Do you know what the Golden Rule is?"

"I really thought I would hear, 'Yes,'" Judge Mazur recalls. "When I was a kid, you saw the Golden Rule on every ruler in school. It was everywhere."

But the teen had no clue. Since that day, Mazur has put the same question before no fewer than 2,500 troubled youths in his court. At most, a dozen – less than one half of one percent – have been able to recite the simple words about doing unto others as you would have them do unto you.

Mazur believes the malaise begins with a society that has become too smart, sophisticated, and cynical, and that is now paying the price for its arrogance. While the teens Mazur sees in court are from particularly troubled circumstances, a quick survey of the American landscape shows that even people with the skills and opportunities to attain the top levels of business, politics, and other arenas, often do so with no grounding in the values that at least ostensibly guided human interrelations in past decades.

"For those willing to listen, it's amazing how much wisdom there is in old trite phrases that people don't like to use any more," Mazur says. On the wall of his office is a needlepoint embroidered by his great grandmother with the words: "Do right, and fear no man."

"To me, it says that, once you establish that you're following your conscience, don't hesitate to be strong in your convictions," Mazur says. "I get a stalwart feeling from it. The wind doesn't bow you."

In a world bent on short-term gain and mutual exploitation, it's too easy to sneer when Mazur articulates the guiding philosophy in his life: being considerate. "It sounds altruistic and friendly and innocent, almost naïve," Mazur says. "On the contrary, consideration of others is a source of tremendous strength and even power.

"It's not about altruism; it's about what works. I've always used being considerate as a weapon."

Mazur is talking about a weapon for understanding others in a way that allows all parties to achieve their goals, a collective win-win. "I use considerateness in such a way that I can figure out what you want, maybe even before you have." he says. "It makes my life easier in a multitude of ways. If I can understand what you're thinking, what motivates you and how far you're willing to go, I know what I'll have to do next. I can eliminate dealing with you if it's not going to be effective. I can put you out of the picture. But if I can see there's any sort of meeting place, we can get to that place very quickly."

The second of eight children in a family of modest means in Grand Prairie, Texas during the 1950s and 60s, Mazur saw the power of such philosophy early on. To be heard, and to get something he wanted, required understanding things from his parents' point of view. "When my father came home from work, I would meet him at the door with his beer, his slippers, and his newspaper. He'd just smile and sit down and it wouldn't be long before I could ask for something within reason. He'd laugh about it, but I always got what I wanted."

It was not cynical manipulation. Mazur was simply willing to provide something that would make his father happy enough to reciprocate.

After his father died, Mazur helped support his family while putting himself through college and law school as a bellman for a Dallas hotel. After law school, he returned to Grand Prairie, served as a municipal judge part time, and opened his own private law practice. By honing his listening skills – listening to words, thoughts, and feelings – he advanced his career.

Considerateness is no easy art. The hardest part is in how you interpret what you hear and how you put it all into action. The process demands time, patience, and practice. "People don't like to look very far down the road. This is not the kind of thing where you get the payoff on the first move," says Mazur. "When you lie back and try to truly understand the other side, it takes awhile…. If you do it often enough, you get better at it."

As a juvenile court judge, and as a volunteer with such organizations as Do the Write Thing, a national program aimed at encouraging personal responsibility and nonviolence among young people, Mazur works hard to instill old values in new people. As Mazur points out, and as forward thinking leaders in all businesses and professions understand, adhering to values is a gift to oneself – and the Golden Rule is a tool the world's best dealmakers are the first to use.

Each leader we interviewed for this book surprised us, challenged our assumptions, and shed new light on aspects of leadership from communicating a global vision to handling crises effectively.

There's no significance to the fact that our rules happen to number 40. The fact that, time and space permitting, we could have gone on interviewing forward-thinking leaders indefinitely, reinforces a salient point about leadership. It is not carved in stone with 10 inviolable commandments. It is a quality that suggests infinite challenges. It is a way of *being*, and subject to constant and often dizzying change.

Many of the principles we have explored are ageless. Time has not dimmed the importance of the Golden Rule, and honesty is still honesty, whether the message is delivered via parchment or cyberspace. Courage is courage. If more financial leaders during the financial meltdown of late 2008 and 2009 had shown the decisive leadership of J.P. Morgan during a similar crisis a century earlier, they and their industry might not now be feeling the ongoing wrath of an embittered world.

Just as surely, though, each new generation must reinterpret and adapt leadership principles to the needs and peculiarities of its own age. The bankers who huddled in Morgan's New York mansion to save the American financial system would be shocked by our current age in which government has assumed a direct role in business matters, and in which news is disseminated, not by a handful of reporters waiting outside their doors, but by millions of self-appointed lay Internet scribes ready to pounce at the barest whiff of crisis. How those men would have responded to the pressures of our time is a matter of conjecture, but one thing is abundantly clear: the nation has never been in greater need of strong, enlightened business leadership than at this moment.

In this historical context, we've looked at leadership from the macro perspective of decision making that affects thousands of employees and millions of customers. We've likewise focused at minute levels of brain chemistry to see how and why people behave the way they do during crisis, and what leaders can do in response to help shape and guide behavior. We've seen a decorated naval commander and carrier pilot struggle with the challenges of leadership in a business environment and find the business world an even greater challenge than leading men into battle.

We've seen many ways in which leadership is counterintuitive: how coercive displays of power may establish one's authority while weakening one's ability to lead; and how the best leaders are the ones who make their employees *want* to produce. We've seen the consequences of failed leadership as executives cower or vainly attack their attackers.

Most important, we've seen the extraordinary possibilities that great leadership can unleash. We hope this book has given you some ideas directly applicable to your own company and your own challenges, and has helped energize you for the new world ahead.

INDEX
of persons and companies